Table of Contents

Keys to Living a Blessed Life © Angela Hood, 2018.

All rights reserved.

No part of this publication may be reproduced or transmitted in any form or by any means without express permission from the publisher.

All scriptures are taken from the American King James Version of the Bible.

Printed in the United States.

www.angelahood.com

Acknowledgements

All Scripture is taken from the New King James Version of the Bible, unless otherwise noted.

I want to thank my family, husband Bishop Hood and my children Elijah and Angelica, thank you for understanding and putting up with mom's busy schedule. To Dynasty and Kuadir, I love you both dearly and it's been a blessing to have you in my life.

To LaQueisa Boyd for your continuous reminder and push to finish this project.

The Enrichment Center—your words of encouragement and support have been a blessing to me in so many ways. Words cannot explain how honored I am to be called your pastor; may God's blessing rest upon you always.

Finally, I would like to acknowledge and thank everyone who has supported me in this project

Background

One of the greatest dangers of studying the Bible is the possibility of taking items out of context. When this happens, Scripture is interpreted based on how it is understood at the moment, instead of understanding each text in its proper context. Well-intending believers run the risk of interpreting each Scripture as stand-alone, instead of comparing Scripture with Scripture. To discover the whole truth of God's Word, the Bible student must look at the Word in its entirety. While it is possible for believers to receive teaching or encouragement from individual verses of the Scripture, it is critical to be sure that what is taken away from each individual verse is in line with the whole of God's Word.

The book of 2 Chronicles is often overlooked. On the surface, it is not as exciting or as insightful as other books, so readers typically skim over it or ignore it altogether. On the other hand, 2 Chronicles 7:14 is one of the most oft-quoted verses in Scripture:

> ... if My people who are called by My name will humble themselves, and pray and seek My face, and turn from their wicked ways, then I will hear from heaven, and will forgive their sin and heal their land.

In the middle of this largely ignored book, we find a golden text. Most Bible students know this one verse, but have little knowledge of its context– how this verse fits into the whole book of 2 Chronicles or the entire story of the Bible. Notice that the verse begins with a lowercase letter because verse 14 starts in the middle of a sentence – the middle of a thought.

This book will focus in depth on 2 Chronicles 7:14, but it is impossible to understand what God is really saying in that verse without understanding the larger context.

The Past

The book of 2 Chronicles is located in what is known as the Old Testament (or Old Covenant, or First Testament). The Old Testament opens with the creation of the world. From the very beginning, God has wanted a deep, intimate, trusting relationship with humanity. However, humanity rejected God from the very beginning. Knowing this would be the case, God's matchless grace was demonstrated here by the plan he set into motion even before the world began. A plan of redemption would be necessary in order for this relationship God desired to have with mankind to be restored. He knew that humanity would reject him and require redemption to be able to enter into a relationship with a Holy God.

God could have created humans who did not have the ability to sin and choose their own desires over his will. He could have made people who worshipped him wholeheartedly from the very beginning; but he did not want robots to serve him. He wanted people who wanted him. He wanted people who would serve him by choice. He wanted people who would choose of their own free will, to love him.

God found such a person in Abraham. When God chose Abraham, he promised to protect and provide for him and his descendants forever. He promised three things to Abraham: land, many descendants and that they would be blessed and also be a blessing to the entire world.

"Now the Lord had said to Abram:

'Get out of your country, from your family and from your father's house, to a land that I will show you. I will make you a great nation; I will bless you, and

make your name great; and you shall be a blessing. I will bless those who bless you, and I will curse him who curses you;
And in you all the families of the earth shall be blessed.' (Genesis 12:1-3)

Though Abraham's descendants did not always keep their end of the bargain, God remained faithful to his promise. Abraham's family grew into an entire nation of people – the nation of Israel. God delivered them from slavery and faithfully led them to the Promised Land. When Israel desired to have a physical leader they could see, hear and touch like the pagan nations around them had, God granted their request and chose judges and kings to lead them. For thousands of years, God remained faithful to His covenant. God blessed Israel, and Israel has been a blessing; it is through Israel we have our Messiah and the Holy Scriptures.

In the time detailed by 2 Chronicles, Israel was established in the Promised Land. King David was about to die, so he passed the crown and the covenant with God to his son, Solomon. David was Israel's most beloved king – a tender warrior who showed his people what it meant to both fight for God and to worship Him.

One of David's greatest desires was to build a Temple for God, a permanent dwelling place for him. The nation of Israel started as a nomadic people. The religious center for the nation had been the Tabernacle, a tent that was easily transported. For David, it was an insult to God that God's people, whom he faithfully led, would build permanent dwellings for themselves but find nothing wrong with allowing God to live in a tent. God, however, had other plans and refused to allow David to be the one to build a permanent Temple for His presence.

Instead, the task of building the Temple fell on Solomon, David's son. The first chapters of 2 Chronicles describe the planning for and building of the Temple. No expense was spared in the construction of God's House. Although it was not a large building, it was extravagantly decorated.

The Bible's description of the Temple King Solomon built suggests that the inside ceiling was 180 feet long, 90 feet wide, and 50 feet high. The highest point on the Temple was about 20 stories. Before the Temple stood a porch corresponding the width of the temple. The Temple was built with stones prepared away from the worksite at the quarry. Because everything was prepared and sized at the quarry, the worksite itself was quiet.

The roof was made of cedar, but the whole house was overlaid with gold. Two bronze pillars stood before the door to the inside of the Temple, and a bronze laver (a giant bowl filled with water), rested on the back of 12 oxen for the priests to bathe in. This was to keep the priests ceremonially clean. An altar of sacrifice also stood in this area, overlaid in gold.

The building contained two rooms. The first, called the Holy Place, was thirty feet high, thirty feet wide and sixty feet long. It contained ten golden tables, ten golden lampstands and one altar of incense. At the end of this area was the Holy of Holies, or "Most Holy Place," of which only the high priest could enter and that only once a year on Yom Kippur, or the Day of Atonement. On this day, the priest would sprinkle the blood of the sacrifice on the altar and the doors of the most holy place, cleansing the people's sins for one year. This Most Holy Place housed the two tablets of the Ten Commandments inside the Ark of Covenant as well as Aaron's rod and a jar of manna.

To appreciate Solomon's temple, consider the literal temple as a type or shadow pointing to the antitype, or reality, which is a spiritual temple. The apostle Paul wrote in the New Testament of believers' bodies as a temple: "Know ye not that ye are the temple of God, and that the Spirit of God dwelleth in you?" (1 Corinthians 3:16, 17). Peter also likened individual church members to living stones: "Ye also as living stones, are built up a spiritual house" (1 Peter 2:5). Immediately our minds are directed toward the literal house or temple Solomon built. A stone building of any size in Biblical times had a cornerstone, which became the foundation for the walls and the building's starting point. This stone beautifully pictures the great antitypical stone, our Lord Jesus: "Behold, I lay in Zion for a foundation a stone, a tried stone, a precious corner stone, a sure foundation" (Isaiah 28:16). Each stone was connected to that firm foundation. The Most Holy place looks towards our eternal dwelling place with God, which Christ entered as our High Priest and sacrificed when he was crucified, his blood cleansing his people from their sins once and for all:

> *Not with the blood of goats and calves, but with His own blood He entered the Most Holy Place once for all, having obtained eternal redemption. (Hebrews 9:12)*

Everything about the temple was symbolic of God's work as redeemer, and everything pointed to Christ. Christ is our cornerstone, the foundation of our faith, and we are the spiritual temple of God, built on Christ.

In spite of the literal temple's opulence, even Solomon understood that no earthly building was truly sufficient to house God.

> *And the Temple which I build will be great, for our God is greater than all gods. But who is able to build Him a Temple, since heaven and the heaven of heavens cannot contain Him? Who am I then, that I should build Him a Temple, except to burn sacrifice before Him? (2 Chronicles 2:5-6)*

The purpose of the Temple was not to *contain* God – for God cannot be contained. The purpose was to give the people *a place to meet* God. The Temple did not provide a greater *amount* of God's presence but a greater *awareness* of and *access* to God's presence. Ultimately, David knew even Solomon was not the one who would build God's house, writing in Psalm 127: "Unless the LORD builds the house, those who build it labor in vain."

David looked forward to a time he could not yet see, a time where God would once again dwell forever among his people. God alone would build the true Temple of God: his people, the church. Solomon's temple was but a picture, or type of church.

When construction was complete, Solomon hosted a worship celebration to dedicate the Temple (2 Chronicles 6). The people offered a huge number of sacrifices to God and when they were finished, the glorious presence of God filled the Temple. Solomon ended the festivities with a speech, combining a beautiful sermon to the people with a prayer to God. All that remained to be spoken was a message from God himself.

The Promise
2 Chronicles 6 records Solomon's prayer and the seventh chapter contains God's response:

Then the Lord appeared to Solomon by night, and said to him: "I have heard your prayer, and have chosen this place for Myself as a house of sacrifice. When I shut up heaven and there is no rain, or command the locusts to devour the land, or send pestilence among My people, if My people who are called by My name will humble themselves, and pray and seek My face, and turn from their wicked ways, then I will hear from heaven, and will forgive their sin and heal their land. Now My eyes will be open and My ears attentive to prayer made in this place. For now I have chosen and sanctified this house, that My name may be there forever; and My eyes and My heart will be there perpetually.

"As for you, if you walk before Me as your father David walked, and do according to all that I have commanded you, and if you keep My statutes and My judgments, then I will establish the throne of your kingdom, as I covenanted with David your father, saying, 'You shall not fail to have a man as ruler in Israel.'

"But if you turn away and forsake My statutes and My commandments which I have set before you, and go and serve other gods, and worship them, then I will uproot them from My land which I have given them; and this house which I have sanctified for My name I will cast out of My sight, and will make it a proverb and a byword among all peoples.

"And as for this house, which is exalted, everyone who passes by it will be astonished and say, 'Why has the LORD done thus to this land and this house?' Then they will answer, 'Because they forsook the LORD God of their fathers, who brought them out of the land of Egypt, and embraced other gods, and worshiped them and served them; therefore He has brought all this calamity on them.'"

Interestingly, God waited until Solomon was alone before he answered. While part of God's answer dealt with all of the people, part was reserved for Solomon alone as king. God's response included both a national promise and a personal promise. This book will focus on the national promise since the personal promise is exclusive to Solomon.

God began this promise to the nation of Israel with three *when* statements:

> *WHEN I shut up heaven so there is no rain . . .*
> *WHEN pestilence comes . . .*
> *WHEN locusts devour the land...*

How gracious God is to give his people a way back to him before they have even wandered away. God knew in advance that his people would break his heart, but he still gave them the opportunity to live a blessed life. Fortunately for us, these promises and principles are not reserved strictly for the nation of Israel. As believers, we share in these same promises of God.

God knows his people well. He knows they are human and often of little faith, and need to know the reward before he considers taking the risk. See, most people are willing to do just about anything if the return is valuable enough. Kids will study in exchange for stickers. Teenagers will do chores in order to get the keys to the car. They won't do the work without a reward!

While that truth may annoy most parents and teachers, it is a truth carried into adulthood that needs to be worked out on a daily basis. How many people would get up each and every day and go to places of employment without knowing the salary or hourly wage they will receive upon completion? It is a basic law of human nature that transcends age: people want to know if the wage is worth the work.

It is a truth that God in his grace works with too. That is why he let his children in on the prize and not just the commands. That is also why this book will be a little "backwards." 2 Chronicles 7:14 is a basic IF/THEN sentence. To see the treasures God is offering those that trust him, it's necessary to look at the THEN statements first. Before looking at God's expectations, consider what the reward is. Before becoming overwhelmed with the IF commands, meditate on the lavish gifts God offers his children. This will help prepare believers to count the cost and determine if the blessing is worth the battle.

What THEN promises does God make to his children?

I will hear from heaven, and will forgive their sin and heal their land. Now My eyes will be open and My ears attentive to prayer made in this place. For now I have chosen and sanctified this house, that My name may be there forever; and My eyes and My heart will be there perpetually. (2 Chronicles 7:14b-16)

First, God will hear. God will give his attention to his people. Second, God will forgive. He accepts his children.
Third, God will heal. He gives abundantly.

God promises that when these things happen, then he makes his presence known to his people. His name, eyes, ears and heart will be with them continually. The fact that God's presence is constant and people will be able to experience God's presence as a daily reality.

God did not begin with an IF statement because he knew the Israelites would disobey and once they disobeyed, discipline would be required. He knows the same of us. The WHEN statements are warnings; God knew they would sin, and made sure they knew it, too.

After the WHEN comes an IF. God specified that Israel would disobey and turn away from him – that is a statement of fact, not speculation. Whether they came back to him or not was a choice. *If My people who are called by My name . . .* God always leaves the option open to come back to him, but he clearly outlined four things that he expects his people to do when they return:

If we...
HUMBLE PRAY
SEEK
REPENT

1. *Humble themselves*
2. *Pray*
3. *Seek his face*
4. *Turn from their wicked ways*

Fortunately, that is not the end of the promise. Even though God does not really owe people anything, including the opportunity to come back to him, he graciously goes beyond mercy and ends with a THEN clause. IF the people come back to God on his terms, THEN this activates the healing of their land. This particular promise was conditional upon their obedience. He will:

1. *HEAR from heaven*
2. *FORGIVE their sin*
3. *HEAL their land*

> Then God
> Will...
> **HEAR**
> **FORGIVE**
> **HEAL**

The Point

Many who are new to the Bible bypass the Old Testament and focus on the New Testament since that is the part of the Bible in which Jesus appears. That is perfectly fine for a new convert, but so many truths are missed if a believer continues to neglect the meat of the Old Testament. Commentator Ray Stedman argues: "These Old Testament books, in exquisitely accurate pictures, show us truths in the spiritual kingdom of our own lives."[1] In other words, the Old Testament physically demonstrates what the New Testament spiritually teaches.

> These Old Testament books, in exquisitely accurate pictures, show us truths in the spiritual kingdom of our own lives.
> **-Ray Stedman**

Both the Tabernacle and the Temple are reflected in a believer's relationship with God. Because of Jesus' sacrifice, believers no longer have a temporary, movable relationship with God (represented by the Tabernacle). Instead, they enjoy a permanent, intimate relationship with God (represented by the Temple). In fact, the New Testament points out that followers of Jesus are the Temple of God's Holy Spirit who lives in them; they belong to him and no longer belong to themselves (1 Corinthians 6:19). Just as the Temple marked a new beginning for the nation of Israel, so God's indwelling Holy Spirit marks a new beginning in our Christian lives – the old has gone, the new has come (2 Corinthians 5:17).

Once God moves in, what happens? God is aware that believers will continue to mess up. There will still be times when sin and disobedience traps people, in spite of his indwelling Spirit. It is not a matter of *if* but *when*. Unlike the Israelites, Christians do not lose their relationship with God when they sin against him because we have a Temple relationship, not a Tabernacle relationship. We do however break our fellowship with God when we sin. Sin breaks his heart and creates a wall between him and his children. Sin creates a temporary barrier.

The good news is: WHEN that happens, believers have an IF. God's children have the option of coming back to him – just as the Israelites did. And even better – a THEN always follows an IF! God is faithful even when His children are not. IF people return on his terms, THEN he stands waiting with open arms to receive them back into fellowship, ready to pour amazing blessings into their lives.

*WHEN... IF... THEN...*What a beautiful promise!

Introduction

WHEN... IF... THEN...

The beautiful promise in 2 Chronicles 7:14 is also a wonderful gift. In the space of a few words, God laid out the plan for living a blessed life. The instructions are plain...there is no need to wonder what he meant or guess what he wants. He clearly explained how people can live in the abundant blessing that comes from his presence.

1. He gave a *REMINDER*: "WHEN you turn away . . ."
2. He gave a *RETURN*: "IF My people . . ."
3. And He gave a *REWARD*: "THEN I will . . ."

How gracious God is to provide a way back to him – along with a treasure on top of that – before we have even wandered from him! God knows in advance that his children will break his heart, but he still offers us the opportunity to live a blessed life.

REMIND
RETURN
REWARD

Because God created us, He knows us very well. He knows that we have a "what's in it for me?" mentality before we consider taking a risk. The reward system is a basic law of human motivation: *decide if the wage is worth the work.*

By and large, people are disinclined to work on "spec." The reward must be displayed in advance. The "carrot and stick" approach may be a lot of work for parents, teachers, and managers but it works- in business, education and behavior modification. It is a "workaday" truth, a truth that God himself utilizes. This is why he lets his people in on the prize (blessings here, heaven later) and not only the commands.

As mentioned earlier, this book is written "backwards." While 2 Chronicles 7:14 is a basic IF/THEN sentence, this work examines the THEN statements first. That way, the treasures God offers are presented *first*. Before God's expectations are examined, the rewards will be displayed. Before the reader is overwhelmed with the IF commands, they will first discover the lavish gifts God offers his children.

2 Chronicles is not the only book of the Bible where this plays out. In the New Testament, Christ commanded his

God HEARS
God FORGIVES
God HEALS

disciples to count the cost and determine if the blessing is worth the battle:

> *If any man come to me, and hate not his father, and mother, and wife, and children, and brethren, and sisters, yea, and his own life also, he cannot be my disciple. And whosoever doth not bear his cross, and come after me, cannot be my disciple. For which of you, intending to build a tower, sitteth not down first, and counteth the cost, whether he have sufficient to finish it? Lest haply, after he hath laid the foundation, and is not able to finish it, all that behold it begin to mock him, saying, This man began to build, and was not able to finish. Or what king, going to make war against another king, sitteth not down first, and consulteth whether he be able with ten thousand to meet him that cometh against him with twenty thousand? Or else, while the other is yet a great way off, he sendeth an ambassage, and desireth conditions of peace. So likewise, whosoever he be of you that forsaketh not all that he hath, he cannot be my disciple. (Luke 14:26-33)*

So, what are the THEN promises to God's children?

> *I will hear from heaven, and will forgive their sin and heal their land. Now My eyes will be open and My ears attentive to prayer made in this place. For now I have*

chosen and sanctified this house, that My name may be there forever; and My eyes and My heart will be there perpetually. (2 Chronicles 7:14b-16)

1. God will *HEAR*. We have His ATTENTION.
2. God will *FORGIVE*. We have His ACCEPTANCE.
3. God will *HEAL*. We have His ABUNDANCE.

In the following chapters and exercises, each IF/THEN statement will be examined in more detail to discover God's wage in response to work.

Then I Will . . .

Chapter 1:

Hear From Heaven

When God *Hears*, We Have His *Attention*.

Now it happened in the process of time that the king of Egypt died. Then the children of Israel groaned because of the bondage, and they cried out; and their cry came up to God because of the bondage. So God heard their groaning, and God remembered His covenant with Abraham, with Isaac, and with Jacob. And God looked upon the children of Israel, and God acknowledged them. (Exodus 2:23-25)

And the LORD said: "I have surely seen the oppression of My people who are in Egypt, and have heard their cry because of their taskmasters, for I know their sorrows. So I have come down to deliver them out of the hand of the Egyptians, and to bring them up from that land to a good and large land, to a land flowing with milk and honey. (Exodus 3:7-8)

A little boy sat in a restaurant with his father, telling him all about his day at school, going on and on in full detail about lessons, people and playtime. Meanwhile, the father was busy looking at his text messages, checking the time and looking at the people around him. After several minutes, the boy asked, "Daddy, are you listening to me?" "Yep," his dad replied. The little boy grabbed his father's face in both of his hands and made him connect eye-to-eye. "Could you listen with your eyes, please?" the little boy asked his father.

Because of modern technology, humans are capable of "selective" hearing. Society is noisy, and people are confronted with so much information that daily sensory overload is a way of life. People can *hear* something without really *listening* to it. An ambulance can be right behind a driver with their siren blaring, and the driver may never even notice it because they are listening to the radio or talking to someone on their cell phone.

My son desires to be an NBA player and attended a basketball camp hosted by NBA star, Dwayne Wade. Wade gathered the players around and let them in on a key element of basketball greats: the key to becoming a successful basketball player is listening. To be great, learn to listen well.

Some people have quite a talent for drowning out noise – or people – so when they read that God hears from heaven, that promise may not sound like such a big deal. Sure, God hears– but is he really listening?

The Hebrew word for "hear" is *shema*. Shema means, "to hear, listen, obey (grant a request); to hear with attention and interest; to hear (as in judicial cases); to understand."[1] That's a lot of meaning packed into one word! It isn't just about our ears acknowledging a noise. The believer's prayers are not simply background noise to God - quite the opposite! He is listening to us with great interest.

In addition, the word *shema* is in the *qal imperfect tense,* which means that God is *actively* and *continually* listening. His children are always on his mind and in his heart…always! Unlike the father at the table with his son, God never takes a break from listening to his children. This almost sounds too good to be true!

The early chapters of Exodus describe some of the darkest moments in Israel's history. Though no fault of their own, Israel was a nation of slaves, held captive in Egypt for approximately 400 years. As time went on, the labor forced upon them became more and more oppressive. The people were in bondage, and there was no hope in sight. They continued to cry out to God, and God heard their cry.

The word translated *groaned* in Exodus 2:24 is the Hebrew word *anach*. It means "to sigh, groan, gasp, or moan – usually in pain or grief." The word for *cried out* in Exodus 2:23 is *za'aq*. It means, "to call out for help – especially in sorrow or complaint." God heard the suffering of his people, whether their cry was coming to him in actual words or in nonverbal utterances. Even when they could not find the words to express their grief, God heard their cry.

A cry for help, *za'aq*, can be done in a spirit of sorrow or a spirit of complaint. The Israelites initially cried out to God in oppression and suffering, but their cry quickly took on an accusatory tone: *Why did you let this happen, God? Why aren't you stopping this, God? Don't you care, God? Where are you, God? Are you even listening, God?*

Even when God's people doubted His goodness, God still listened. He never became frustrated or annoyed at their whining. He never told them to figure out their own problems. Even when they blamed him, God heard their cry.

When God heard the cry of the Israelites, scripture says he remembered them. At first glance, that may sound like God had forgotten them – that he took a 400-year break from listening to his people. If we look closer, however, we will see the original meaning for this word means something profoundly different.

The Hebrew word *zakar* actually means, "to consider." God heard the Israelite's cry and considered it. He recalled the vow he had made to Israel through Abraham, and acted according to his covenant promises, especially in a way evident to his people.

God is sovereign over all things, and never loses his perfect compilation of the facts (Hebrews 4:13).

That might not sound very comforting – but keep in mind that God is God. He was not obligated to even listen to them, so he certainly did not have to consider them, BUT he did. In their time of suffering, God considered his people. He called to mind the fact that he had a covenant with them. He played out the best course of action for them and, unbeknownst to Israel, for the rest of mankind.

After God considered Israel, he *acknowledged* them. Other translations use the word *respected* rather than *acknowledged*. The word *acknowledge* is preferable because it suggests that God understood and agreed. Many times when people are suffering, they really just need someone to acknowledge their pain and their right to be upset. God did that for his people. He acknowledged their right to complain and to ask for help. He agreed with their frustrations.

> GOD
> ... SEES HIS PEOPLE
> ...HEARS THEIR CRY
> ...KNOWS THEIR SORROWS
> ...HAS COME TO DELIVER

The story, however, does not stop there. Further along in Exodus 3:7-8, God repeats his acknowledgement: *I have seen my people. I have heard their cry. I know their sorrows. I have come down to deliver them.* He didn't leave them in their sorrow. He came down to deliver them.

I HAVE HEARD. I KNOW. I HAVE COME DOWN TO DELIVER.

When God says, "I will hear from heaven," that is exactly what he means. It is God's way of saying he *goes* with us, he *gets* us and he will *guard* us. The first part of living under the lavish blessing of God is the knowledge that *his attention* is *our possession*.

God Goes With Us

> Before we can enjoy God's presence in our lives, we must accept God's continual presence in our lives as an absolute fact.
>
> -**Beth Moore**

Bible teacher Beth Moore wrote, "Before we can enjoy God's presence in our lives, we must accept God's continual presence in our lives as an absolute fact."[1] Notice that the blessing is *knowing* that the attention of Almighty God is for the child of God's possession. Truthfully, having the attention is a treasure – but only if the believer lives that reality in his or her life. Most Christians behave as though God completely ignores them. Theoretically, we should know that God listens when we talk to him (although sometimes we doubt that too), but most of the time we figure he is too busy to pay attention to our lives. Most Christians believe that he focuses on them only while they are praying or in a worship service. During the times when they are not in prayer, they believe God is occupied elsewhere.

Some Christians see God as a super talented multi-tasker at best. They assume he is juggling 6 billion lives at the same time, putting

---

[1] Breaking Free: 70

some lesser important ones on hold so he can focus on the really important people.

I have a friend (who is obviously not a morning person) who likes to joke that if we get up too early in the morning we are infringing on Europe's time with God. Do you ever feel that way? Do you ever wonder if God is relieved when you go to sleep because that means he gets a break from you for a few hours? Do you ever think God needs time away from you? If so, then you may have an inaccurate concept of God.

> An infinite God can give all of Himself to each of His children. He does not distribute Himself that each may have a part, but to each one He gives all of Himself as fully as if there were no others.
>
> –A.W. Tozer

God does not multi-task. As part of his *"Godness"*, his *omnipotence,* his *omniscience* and his *omnipresence,* he is completely focused on *one* while at the same time, completely focused on *all.* His omnipotence ('omni', meaning "all" and 'potence,' meaning "power") is the condition of being "all powerful." He possesses all the power in the universe. If there is any power, of any kind, anywhere, it belongs to and emanates from God himself. Secondly, his omniscience (meaning "all science", or "all knowledge," is the condition of knowing everything there is to know, whether past, present or future. God's omniscience allows him to be aware, or have knowledge of everything and everyone, everywhere, and at all times. Finally, God's omnipresence (again 'omni' or "all" and 'presence' – you guessed it!) means that he is present everywhere, with everyone, in every place, at all times. Can you see how these three attributes of God allow him to be SO MUCH MORE than just a multi-tasker? If he WAS a super multi-tasker, he would be proving his love toward people in the very act of paying attention to everyone at the same time. But now get this concept – it will change your life . . . God does not have to commit an *act* of paying attention or hearing us. It is not what he *does* that demonstrates his love for us, it is what he *is* that shows how he feels toward us. Do you see what I'm saying? God can do nothing *but* love people because that is who he *is*. He does not simply commit acts of love toward mankind –he *is* love. GOD <u>IS</u> LOVE. It's not just what he does; it's what he *is*. Let that sink in for a minute. Fully understanding this principle erases any doubt that God is listening.

WATERS: TRANSITORY DANGER
RIVERS: OVERFLOWING TROUBLES

A. W. Tozer explains, "An infinite God can give all of himself to each of his children. He does not distribute Himself that each may have a part, but to each one he gives all of himself as fully as if there were no others."[2] In other words, God is not relieved when we go to sleep so that he can get a break from thinking about us! He is thinking and caring for each of his children all the time.

Sometimes it feels like prayers bounce off the ceiling. It seems that God is on the other side of the universe busying himself with someone else's problems. Satan wants believers to feel abandoned by God. He wants to convince his children that their feelings are a bigger reality than the promises in the Bible.

However, those feelings are not true. Here's what believers can count on: God never once forgets anyone, loses track of people, or is too occupied to focus on each person individually. His children have the complete and undivided attention of the Almighty God all the time, whether it feels like it or not. God is with us- that's what *Emmanuel* means. He was with each person five minutes ago, he is with them this

---

[2] Source unknown

very moment and will be with them five minutes from now. He has always been and always will be with his children. Sometimes stepping out in faith is a necessary step for people to realize God has not abandoned them, even if it feels like he has.

Take a moment to enjoy this promise:

> But now, thus says the LORD, who created you, O Jacob, and He who formed you, O Israel: "Fear not, for I have redeemed you; I have called you by your name; You are Mine. When you pass through the waters, I will be with you; and through the rivers, they shall not overflow you. When you walk through the fire, you shall not be burned, nor shall the flame scorch you. For I am the LORD your God, the Holy One of Israel, your Savior." (Isaiah 43:1-3)

Much of scripture delivers God's truth in poetic terms. For instance, the word *water* is symbolic for *transitory danger*. *Rivers* are metaphoric for *overflowing troubles*. *Fire* represents *consuming, destroying war* – whether external or internal. Here's the point: life brings waters, rivers and fire – but God remains near to his children through all of them.

Sometimes we encounter water, or brief but frightening situations. Losing control of a car while driving is terrifying, for example, but only for a moment. As you pass through brief, troubling circumstances, God is there.

Other situations are much more overflowing. It may seem like there are many rushing rivers surrounding a person, leaving them feeling like they are fighting for their very lives. Even then, God is there (omnipresent).

Then there are the fiery trials of life. These times may seem worse because outside circumstances have inside consequences. These are the times when a person may find themselves fighting physically, mentally, emotionally and spiritually. Some fear backing down will mean utter destruction; if they lose the battle that too will mean complete oblivion. However, God's presence never leaves even when it feels like the worst has come. When going through the fire, focus on the fact that *God is there.*

It may be cliché, but nonetheless, it is true: *God didn't promise that life would be easy; He simply promised to be present in the trials of life.* The understanding of his omnipresence guarantees that. Actually, his Word guarantees that; understanding this concept brings assurance.

God told the Israelites they would experience waters, rivers, and fire, but they did not need to be afraid because he knew them, loved them and honored them. Even when the waters rose and the rivers surged, they could be confident in the knowledge that God was with them. He would not let them go. He won't let any of His children walk through troubles alone.

HAVING GOD'S ATTENTION MEANS HE GOES WITH US.

God Gets Us

It is incredibly comforting to know that God goes with us through the best and worst times of life, but that is still not really enough. Fortunately, God agrees. That is why he doesn't just promise to *be with* believers, he also promises to "get," or to understand his children. This is where the attribute mentioned earlier, his omniscience, or "all-knowing," comes in. Notice that one of the definitions of *shema* is "to understand." What an awesome gift it is to know that God Almighty understands his people. He is not shocked or surprised by people's circumstances or reactions to those circumstances. He knows exactly how every circumstance arises, exactly how people feel about them, and exactly what they need to do about them.

David understood that God "got" him, and he appreciated that gift so much that he wrote an entire Psalm to thank God for it. Psalm 139 begins with the assurance that God understands:

> O LORD, You have searched me and known me. You know my sitting down and my rising up; You understand my thought afar off. You comprehend my path and my lying down, and are acquainted with all my ways. (Psalm 139:1-3)

God knows us. God understands us. God comprehends us. God is acquainted with us. He knows our actions. He knows our intentions. He knows our words. He knows our thoughts.

God *gets* us.

But here's the really awesome thought: *God gets us because he searches.* The word *shema* means, "to hear with attention and interest." God finds people fascinating. He finds humankind so interesting that he spends his time searching the inner recesses of our hearts and minds, not just to catch a glimmer of what makes people tick, but also to show us our own selves, that we may know him better also. He does this to demonstrate his complete love and benevolence over our lives.

Maybe it doesn't mean much to know that God gets us, but it means the world to some. God isn't just *stuck* with his children. *He loves us.* He enjoys people's company. He knows exactly what is going on inside of each and every one of his children. We were created in his image and according to his likeness.

HAVING GOD'S ATTENTION MEANS HE GETS US.

God Guards Us

Knowing that God is present is great. Knowing that he gets his children is awesome. But what good is either of those if that is all God does? There is comfort in the knowledge that the Father doesn't leave us alone, but will that knowledge really change anything? Not really - not if we don't grasp that God acts on our behalf.

God doesn't simply sit and listen. God *understands*. But God doesn't just understand- He also *works*. God guards. God protects. God defends. This is his omnipotence in action. God works for our benefit. He doesn't just pass through the waters with us; he holds the waters back from overwhelming us in the current. He has the power to do that. He doesn't just walk through the fire with us; he keeps us from being burned. David realized this awesome truth about God, too. Psalm 139 continues to say:

GOD HELD DAVID'S HAND and, WHEN NECESSARY, GOD PICKED HIM UP and HELD HIM IN HIS ARMS

You have hedged me behind and before, and laid Your hand upon me…Even there Your hand shall lead me, and Your right hand shall hold me. (Psalm 139:5, 10)

God didn't just know David; God guarded David. He didn't simply walk with David; he hedged him about – he surrounded David with safety. God literally laid his hand on David to guide and hold him. Treasure the imagery in that statement: *God held David's hand and when it was necessary, God picked up David and held him completely in his arms.*

There are so many times in life when it may not seem like God is even listening. He seems so far away that it is easy for the enemy to convince people that God doesn't care. But God *does* care. God hears his people cry. God knows what is going on because he has been paying attention the whole time and he always comes through for his people. He acts on behalf of those who love him. Again, this is because of who and what he is. He can do nothing less. We can count on that, even though it may not seem like it is true at this very moment. He is *Emmanuel . . . God with us*. Not *God ignoring us*. Not *God sitting idly by*. Not *God wondering what is going on*. God Almighty is *with, in* and *for* his children.

> For since the beginning of the world men have not heard nor perceived by the ear, nor has the eye seen any God besides You, who acts for the one who waits for Him. (Isaiah 64:4)

HAVING GOD'S ATTENTION MEANS HE GUARDS US.

LIVING UNDER THE LAVISH BLESSING OF GOD

Paul reminded the Church in Rome that nothing can separate the believer from God and his love: not peril, not famine, not distress...nothing. Those things do not have the power to separate us from God. Because they cannot separate us from him, we are "more than conquerors" when those difficult times arise. The way this happens is simple: Christians live in the reality of knowing that God hears them.

> *There is therefore now no condemnation to those who are in Christ Jesus, who do not walk according to the flesh, but according to the Spirit. What then shall we say to these things? If God is for us, who can be against us? He who did not spare His own Son, but delivered him up for us all, how shall he not with him also freely give us all things? Who shall bring a charge against God's elect? It is God who justifies. Who is he who condemns? It is Christ who died, and furthermore is also risen, who is even at the right hand of God, who also makes intercession for us. Who shall separate us from the love of Christ? Shall tribulation, or distress, or persecution, or famine, or nakedness, or peril, or sword? Yet in all these things we are more than*

conquerors through Him who loved us. For I am persuaded that neither death nor life, nor angels nor principalities nor powers, nor things present nor things to come, nor height nor depth, nor any other created thing, shall be able to separate us from the love of God which is in Christ Jesus our Lord. (Romans 8:1, 31-39)

What does it really mean to say, "God hears us?" It is so much more than one may think. It means that we have the undivided attention of Almighty. Let that truth sink in. God – the Creator, Sustainer and Provider of the Universe – pays attention to each of us. But there is more. Having God's attention means God is *with* us…God is on our side. It means God *gets* us, and it means God *protects* us.

Knowing that fact, that God hears, and living the reality of that truth, are two very different things. One is knowledge of the head and the other is knowledge of the heart. Paul said in Romans 8 that he was *persuaded.* He was not *somewhat convinced* and was not *thinking it through.* Paul was persuaded – thoroughly certain – that God was with him regardless of his life circumstances. We also can live under his lavish blessing when we, like Paul, have become convinced of that truth.

I WILL HEAR FROM HEAVEN . . .

I GO WITH YOU. I GET YOU. I GUARD YOU.

Your Turn

1. What does it mean to you personally that God listens to you and hears you?

   _____

   _____

   _____

   _____

   _____

2. Are there times when you feel like God is ignoring you or just doesn't care? If so, describe them.

   _____

   _____

   _____

   _____

   _____

3. What does it mean to you personally to know that God is with you? When does that fact matter to you?

   _____

   _____

   _____

   _____

   _____

What does it mean to you to know that God gets you? When does that fact matter to you?

_____

_____

_____

_____

_____

4. What does it mean to you to know that God acts on your behalf? When has God come through for you in the past?

_____

_____

_____

_____

_____

Chapter 2:

Forgive Their Sin

When God *Forgives*, We Have His *Acceptance.*

He got into a boat, crossed over, and came to His own city. Then behold, they brought to Him a paralytic lying on a bed. When Jesus saw their faith, He said to the paralytic, "Son, be of good cheer; your sins are forgiven you." And at once some of the scribes said within themselves, "This Man blasphemes!"

But Jesus, knowing their thoughts, said, "Why do you think evil in your hearts? For which is easier, to say, 'Your sins are forgiven you,' or to say, 'Arise and walk'? But that you may know that the Son of Man has power on earth to forgive sins"—then He said to the paralytic, "Arise, take up your bed, and go to your house." And he arose and departed to his house. (Matthew 9:1-7)

I love the stories of Jesus calming the sea, healing the lepers and raising the dead. I love his teachings and contemplating how he interacted with people. It is easy to get caught up in these awesome and miraculous stories. It is easy to be so amazed by his power over disease and death that we lose sight of what Jesus really came to do: seek and save the lost. Jesus accomplished many things during his time on earth, but the reason for his life was his death. Other people could teach us those truths. Other people could intercede for us. Other people could heal us. *Only the Son of God could save us.*

Giving a lame man the ability to walk again is an amazing miracle. Taking away someone's sin, however, is even greater. It is easy to lose sight of the fact that the only reason Jesus performs his other miracles at all is to prove his power over sin. Someone else could have healed the man, but only Jesus has the power to forgive.

I think we lose sight of the amazing gift (and miracle) of forgiveness. One reason for that is that we underestimate our own sin. We excuse a lot of our behavior that God calls abominable. We compare ourselves to other people to make ourselves feel better. "Sure, I may lie or gossip, but I don't do any really *bad* stuff- I don't steal or kill." We measure up our sins against the sins of others instead of using Christ as our measuring rod of righteousness.

We also overestimate our own ability. Whether I like the truth or not, the reality is that the *only* way I can find forgiveness is through the blood of Jesus Christ. There is nothing I can do, nothing I can say, that will make me good.

I may underestimate my sin or overestimate my ability, but God does neither. In his eyes, sin is filth, and my righteousness is as dirty rags. Have you ever tried to sterilize something with a filthy rag? It doesn't work. According to Scripture, that is the best we can do when it comes to our sin- we just move the mess around. But there is forgiveness in the arms of God, and his forgiveness is more than fancy words or a fleeting feeling. When God forgives, he *atones, accepts* and *adopts.*

God Atones our Sins

The Son of Man came to seek and to save that which was lost. (Luke 19:10, Amplified Bible).

Let's turn now to an interesting character named Zaccheus. Beginning in Luke 15 through Jesus' calling Zaccheus by name in Luke 19, a common theme is woven in the pages of the scripture. Jesus has just given a sermon to tax collectors and sinners, teaching them about the nature of sin. The tax collectors, or publicans, were Jews who had been hired by the Roman government to collect taxes (at a sizable markup) from their fellow Israelites. They were regarded as traitors against their race, putting them in their own special category of sinners. Luke describes their attitude towards Jesus, saying, "The Pharisees and the scribes complained, saying 'this man receives or welcomes sinners and eats with them'" (Luke 15:2). They were looking for an opportunity to besmirch Christ's character, implying that if Jesus receives and eats with sinners then he must be one also. The sinfulness of the audience was obvious, so Jesus presents his teaching in terms they would have been quite familiar with: a wandering sheep, lost and misplaced money, and a rebellious son. Jesus wanted to convey the message that *every* soul was worth saving.

GOD IS NOT STINGY ABOUT MEETING OUR NEEDS.

It is important to know that Jewish culture in Biblical times was a shame verses honor-driven society. Shame and honor was used in a way that developed nothing short of a caste system. The primary reason people did *anything* good was to seek honor for oneself, all the while avoiding shame. So it is interesting that Jesus uses parables to challenge the Pharisees where they are failing most: their lives were all about outward appearance and honor.

Jesus starts with the parable of the lost sheep, describing a shepherd who has lost one of his 100 sheep. Jesus questions the Pharisees, asking, 'What shepherd would not go out to find his lost sheep, and rejoice when he finds it?' Jesus concludes that there will be more rejoicing in heaven over one sinner who repents than over ninety-nine righteous people who do not need to repent. But Jesus, knowing the sinners' hearts, keeps going. He tells another parable of a woman who loses a coin and searches until she finds it (Luke 15:8-10). Jesus' point in this parable is that mere people will put much effort into searching for something that has little eternal value! How much more will our heavenly Father search and seek out the lost souls of humanity and rejoice when they repent and turn to God. Jesus was turning his listeners understanding of things upside down. The Pharisees saw themselves as being the loved and righteous of God, and the "sinners" as filth. Jesus uses the Pharisees prejudices against them, but encourages the sinners with one clear message: God has a tender, personal concern and joyous love for his people who are lost in sin, and he rejoices over each and every one that turns back to him in humble repentance.

Next, Jesus tells his audience the parable of the lost son, which symbolizes the forgiveness of God when we are reconciled to him through Christ Jesus. A young man demands his share of his father's estate, taking it and squandering it on the things of this world. It was not a loving thing to do, as it was comparable to wishing his father dead. Instead of rebuking his son, the father patiently grants the son's request. The young man loses everything, and finds himself destitute and working for a stranger, feeding pigs. He realizes he has no right to claim any blessing upon the return to his father's household, but decides to come home and fall at his father's feet, begging for forgiveness and mercy.

The father, waiting and hoping for his son's return, not only forgives him, but restores back to him the full privilege of being his father's son. The prodigal son's older brother is not the least bit relieved that his younger brother has returned home; in fact, he is so consumed with issues of justice and equity that he fails to see or even care about his brother's repentance and return. The older brother's jealous anger takes root in his heart, making him unable to show any love or compassion towards his brother.

The tax collectors and sinners who gathered together to hear Jesus represent the lost son who was once with the father and left, but later came back to the father. The Pharisees and scribes represent the older brother who was so caught up in his self-righteousness that he could not rejoice in his brother's return. The parable of the prodigal son is a picture of God letting a sinner go his own way, but being ready to receive him with open arms when he repents and returns home.

Then, in chapter 16, Jesus turns to his disciples and builds on the reaction of the unforgiving older son and tells a story about a steward and a rich man. The parable begins with a rich man relieving his steward of his duties for mismanaging his master's resources. The master is most likely unaware that the steward has actually been *dishonest* with his money; he hasn't simply mismanaged it. Realizing he will be out of a job, the steward makes some final shrewd deals with his master's money before he is out on the street, reducing the master's debt to a few other people in exchange for a place to live. Surprisingly, when the master realizes what the wicked servant has done, he commends him for his shrewdness. At first, this seems a bit odd. It seems like Jesus was approving the unjust steward's conduct.

However, Jesus was illustrating what God's indescribable forgiveness looks like. If the shrewd master can forgive his unjust servant, how much more does God forgive us of our sins? This parable gives insight into the sinfulness of man and the vast mercy of God.

Jesus' message of forgiveness then shifts to an explanation of how some people try to justify themselves before men with money, but God knows the true intent of the heart. The Pharisees placed a high priority on financial security. But Jesus tells the Pharisees in Luke 16: 15, what is highly esteemed among men is an abomination in the sight of God. Jesus wanted the Pharisees and scribes to understand that leading up to John the Baptist, the Jews had the protection of the law. Then John the Baptist appears on the scene, proclaiming that the kingdom of God has been preached and *everyone*, tax collectors and sinners alike, are welcomed into it. Jesus was making it very clear that he is no respecter of persons and everyone has an opportunity to be saved. In verse Luke 16:19-31, God uses the story of the rich man and Lazarus to explain a principle about money and how it does not truly protect anyone.

After this, he returns to continue teaching his disciples, traveling through Galilee and Samaria where he heals some lepers and answers some theological questions from the Pharisees. Again, his conclusion is that money provides zero protection against the judgment of God.

In chapter 18, Jesus teaches the disciples a very direct lesson about prayer: God is not stingy about meeting our needs. Then he begins teaching particular groups of lost people. He addresses self-righteousness versus humbly confessing sin (9-14). He instructs his disciples to be sure to concentrate on the spiritual vulnerability of children, implying that childhood is the best time to come to God (15-17). As a result of meeting the rich young ruler and the disciples' reaction to that meeting, Jesus explains that the barriers to God or things we love more than God, must be removed from our lives in order to gain eternal life (18-30). He explains to his disciples that very soon, they would be without his physical presence and they would feel lost (31-34). He then heals a blind man, someone who was completely lost, both physically and spiritually (35-42).

Finally, in chapter 19, we meet Zaccheus (19:1-10). Zaccheus was a chief tax collector and a rich man who wanted to see who Jesus was. Clearly, the Spirit of God was calling Zaccheus to know Jesus, as "no man can see me unless the father draws him" (John 6:44). But Zaccheus was not a very tall man, apparently not even tall enough to see Jesus over the crowd. He could only hear him, so he ran ahead and climbed up a sycamore tree to catch a glimpse of the person who taught about salvation for all. Zaccheus was intrigued and drawn to God. Zaccheus had heard, possibly from a business associate that Jesus spoke of salvation even for tax collectors. Zaccheus repented and believed in what Jesus said; Jesus restored him, not only to renewed status as a Jew, but more importantly, as a saved man. Here is where Jesus makes his pronouncement, explaining everything that happened in Luke 15:1-19:9. It was his purpose statement, his mission and his reason for being on earth:

*The Son of Man came to **seek** and to **save** that which was lost.*

DEFINITIONS OF CHRIST'S MISSION

Let's begin with Christ's mission, and examine more closely everything he has already said about it. We'll start with simple definitions from the Greek New Testament.

Seek

Seek is kind of a soft word in English. Not so in the original Koine Greek. The word in Luke 19:10 is translated: 1) to seek in order to find; 1a) to seek a thing; 1b) to seek [in order to find out] by thinking, meditating, reasoning, to enquire into; 1c) to seek after, seek for, aim at, strive after; 2) to seek i.e. require, demand; 2a) to crave, demand something from someone.[3] It sounds more serious the way Jesus originally said it. To say that we *crave* something takes it up a notch. Christ's *seeking purpose* is passionate.

---

[3] Online Greek Bible, http://www.greekbible.com/index.php

Save

Save is also a soft-sounding word in the English language, and an unpleasant word because of its financial context. We don't like to save. We like to spend. In Luke, Jesus uses this word referring to a lifeguard or fireman. The Koine Greek is pronounced *sode'-zo*. It means: 1) to save, keep safe and sound, to rescue from danger or destruction; 1a) one (from injury or peril); 1a1) to save a suffering one (from perishing), i.e. one suffering from disease, to make well, heal, restore to health; 1b1) to preserve one who is in danger of destruction, to save or rescue; 1b) to save in the technical biblical sense; 1b1) negatively; 1b1a) to deliver from the penalties of the Messianic judgment; 1b1b) to save from the evils which obstruct the reception of the Messianic deliverance.[4] It adds urgency to a situation, as if the sheep is actually going to die if it isn't found. It implies danger. *Save* means more than rescue; it means that the one being saved is at odds with God Himself.

Lost

Lost, however, is a very fine word in English. It carries the idea of directionless, hopelessness and futility, as in such phrases as *lost love, lost at sea or lost in the woods.* The Greek word is pronounced *ap-ol'-loo-mee.* It means: 1) to destroy 1a) to put out of the way entirely, abolish, put an end to, ruin; 1b) render useless; 1c) to kill; 1d) to declare that one must be put to death; 1e) to devote or give over to eternal misery in hell; 1f) to perish, to be lost, ruined, destroyed; 2) to destroy; 2a) to lose.[5] That which is lost must be sought and saved because death, danger, damnation and destruction lurk on every horizon.

---

4 Ibid.
5 Ibid.

DESCRIPTIONS OF LOSTNESS

The three parables in Luke are actually different aspects of the same
idea: *God cares about lost people - no matter how they are lost.*

GOD CARES
ABOUT LOST
PEOPLE – NO
MATTER HOW
THEY ARE LOST

The sheep was lost because of foolish wandering (4-7)

What man of you, having an hundred sheep, if he lose one of them, doth not leave the ninety and nine in the wilderness, and go after that which is lost, until he find it? And when he hath found it, he layeth it on his shoulders, rejoicing. And when he cometh home, he calleth together his friends and neighbours, saying unto them, "Rejoice with me; for I have found my sheep which was lost." I say unto you, that likewise joy shall be in heaven over one sinner that repenteth, more than over ninety and nine just persons, which need no repentance.

The sheep had no intention of leaving the safety of the fold. This was a slip, a lapse of judgment and simple carelessness. The sheep had no concept of abandoning his shepherd's protection. He simply didn't pay attention. Maybe he just kept following the green grass and never looked up to see that he was alone. Whatever the reason, a careless sheep makes just as good a meal for a wolf as a rebellious one (if there is such a thing as a rebellious sheep) and he'll be just as dead *if* he isn't found.

In order for the sheep to be brought back to safety, the shepherd must leave the remainder of the herd to go and seek the lost sheep. The remaining flock of sheep will have to be by themselves for a while during the shepherd's rescue mission because that is the nature of a shepherd's heart. A shepherd leaves the safety of the group to seek the lost member of the fold.

Often, when Christians wander away from God's safety, it's a *slip*. It's *unintentional*. They don't mean to turn their backs on God, but something else lures their attention away from God and before they knew it, they are out on their own, fair game for the overwhelming temptations of the world. When this happens, pastors and Christian friends have to go looking for them. Sometimes they take a lot of time to salvage, and other believers have to fend for themselves in the group while they are gone.

HOW MANY MEMBERS HAVE STOPPED ATTENDING OUR CHURCHES AND NO ONE EVEN NOTICED?

Sheep also tend to complain when another sheep demands all the attention, and, if they continue in that self-centeredness, they may begin to wander too; and so it goes ...one lost sheep can lead a whole fold of wandering, lost little lambs.

The coin was lost through the neglect of another (8-10)

Either what woman having ten pieces of silver, if she lose one piece, doth not light a candle, and sweep the house, and seek diligently till she find it? And when she hath found it, she calleth her friends and her neighbors together, saying, Rejoice with me; for I have found the piece which I had lost. Likewise, I say unto you, there is joy in the presence of the angels of God over one sinner that repenteth.

The owner of the coins lost 10 percent of her treasure through simple neglect. Maybe she saw the coins and didn't bother to count them but carelessly glanced her way and continued about her business. Perhaps the coin was hard to find because the house was dark and some rubbish needed to be swept away before it could be found.

It's terrible to be gone and have no one notice your absence. It's disheartening when there is so much clutter in life that people's absence goes unnoticed. It's easy to see the shepherd in the first parable as God, but it's difficult to understand the woman as any part of the Godhead. God is never neglectful, and the story implies that *neglect* is the culprit in this story. It's almost as though the lost person represented by this coin was *pushed* out of fellowship. The woman in this story, who must clean her house and bring into light neglected accounts, could be interpreted as Judaism. Judaism is a religion whose leaders came to believe they were too holy for sinners, especially for tax collectors. Judaism was only for *good people*. Sadly, those leaders were perfectly willing for sinners and tax collectors to be punished by God, and were willing to help him along in that journey if opportunity arose.

Even though this story was told to a Jewish audience, it has application for the church today. How many members have stopped attending church with no one even noticing? Until self-centeredness, laziness and darkness is cleared away, it is very likely that churches will continue to lose members because of carelessness.

The son was lost because of his own rebellion (11-32)

And he said, "A certain man had two sons: And the younger of them said to his father, Father, give me the portion of goods that falleth to me. And he divided unto them his living. And not many days after the younger son gathered all together, and took his journey into a far country, and there wasted his substance with riotous living. And when he had spent all, there arose a mighty famine in that land; and he began to be in want. And he went and joined himself to a citizen of that country; and he sent him into his fields to feed swine. And he would fain have filled his belly with the husks that the swine did eat: and no man gave unto him. And when he came to himself, he said, How many hired servants of my father's have bread enough and to spare, and I perish with hunger! I will arise and go to my father, and will say unto him, Father, I have sinned against heaven, and before thee, And am no more worthy to be called thy son: make me as one of thy hired servants.

And he arose, and came to his father. But when he was yet a great way off, his father saw him, and had compassion, and ran, and fell on his neck, and kissed him. And the son said unto him, Father, I have sinned against heaven, and in thy sight, and am no more worthy to be called thy son. But the father said to his servants, Bring forth the best robe, and put it on him; and put a ring on his hand, and shoes on his feet: And bring hither the fatted calf, and kill it; and let us eat, and be merry:

For this my son was dead, and is alive again; he was lost, and is found. And they began to be merry. Now his elder son was in the field: and as he came and drew nigh to the house, he heard music and dancing. And he called one of the servants, and asked what these things meant. And he said unto him, Thy brother is come; and thy father hath killed the fatted calf, because he hath received him safe and sound. And he was angry, and would not go in: therefore came his father out, and intreated him.

And he answering said to his father, Lo, these many years do I serve thee, neither transgressed I at any time thy commandment: and yet thou never gavest me a kid, that I might make merry with my friends: But as soon as this thy son was come, which hath devoured thy living with harlots, thou hast killed for him the fatted calf. And he said unto him, Son, thou art ever with me, and all that I have is thine. It was meet that we should make merry, and be glad: for this thy brother was dead, and is alive again; and was lost, and is found.

Oscar Wilde called this the greatest short story ever written. It contains elements that need little explanation: rebellion, risk, return, restoration and resentment. Every family probably has one of these stories. The lost-ness in this story came about through stubbornness, arrogance, and rebellion. This time, however, no one went seeking. Since the older brother accurately described what the younger brother had been up to, it is possible that he went looking for him and was repulsed at what he saw. He may even have gone to his brother and asked him to come home, receiving scorn in return. Maybe he went home, told his father, saw his father weep, and was filled with contempt for his brother. We can only guess at the details surrounding the story.

Every pastor has seen this type of thing happen. People happily come into the church, but leave when they are challenged or convicted; because their conviction is uncomfortable, they embrace the lure of the world and what they think it can offer. We could say these people *jump* out of their safe zone to see what they've been missing. If they were trained up in the way they should go, they would soon "come to themselves" and then want to come home. Once these folks returns back to the fold, we as pastors rejoice because we have been praying and watching for them and are now overjoyed to see them. All is forgiven. We clothe them with a robe of borrowed righteousness, a ring of relationship and shoes of readiness. However, there is often someone like the older son that *isn't* happy. That person is filled with resentment and self-righteousness, and now *he or she* is the one in danger of being lost.

DUTIES OF THE GODHEAD
The Son Seeks.
Jesus puts this in terms of human nature, and what a person's natural reaction would be. If someone loses something precious, they typically look for it immediately, just as the shepherd did. When he found the

> THE SON SEEKS
> THE SPIRIT SHOWS
> THE FATHER RECEIVES

sheep, he put him up on his shoulders and carried him home. A natural reaction took place: he rejoiced and wanted all his friends to be happy, too. Jesus calls himself our shepherd (John 10). He leads us beside still waters and restores our souls (Psalm 23). Our welfare is his purpose for coming to earth.

The Spirit Shows.

The most natural reaction to finding a lost item is to search for it, and in doing so, we may discern that much clutter has accumulated. It must be cleared away and light must be brought in. When the woman found the coin, she too did what came naturally. She rejoiced and told all her friends about it, and they rejoiced too. The Holy Spirit, because he is holy, points out the clutter of our lives that must be cleaned away in order to make room for the precious lost item. The Holy Spirit, because he leads us into all truth, sheds light on our situation so we can find what we've lost.

The Father Receives.

The father of the rebellious son didn't *seek*; he *waited*. Sheep aren't very smart, and coins have no intellect, emotions or will of their own. The father waited for the world to treat his son the way it naturally does, and for the boy to fall back upon the nature his home life had trained into him. The world used and abused the boy, and the boy got homesick. However, something *unnatural* happened too. When it was time to celebrate, the older brother didn't. In fact, he refused, and he was angry when everyone else celebrated. If his brother came home, he wanted him in the exact status the brother had assigned to himself in order to come home: a servant. The father, however, received what he was waiting for: his *son*. The person who didn't rejoice now stands in danger of rebelling and becoming lost...and so it goes. One rebellious person can create many more.

God is our waiting and patient Father, *all* the time. Even though we are not able by nature to be patient at all times, God has put his Spirit in us who believe in Jesus. This means that his very character is within us. We have his loving-kindness, his gentleness, his ability to forgive and his patience. Rather than responding unnaturally the way the older son responded, we have the ability with the power of his

Spirit in us to put aside our anger and pride and forgive too. We have the ability to wait patiently for family and friends who have turned from God, and perhaps hurt us along the way, to welcome them *back as family*, with no strings attached. God's image in us brings about right thinking, right feelings and right actions.

The older brother probably thought his younger brother finally received what was coming to him. He *should* have to grovel. He *should* have to earn his way back into the family's good graces. Sometimes, when Christians have stumbled, some church members may feel the same way. That attitude, however, reveals an ignorance of the utter helplessness of every wanderer, cast-off or rebel. Paul described us like this:

> *For when we were still **without strength**, in due time Christ died for the **ungodly**. For scarcely for a righteous man will one die; yet perhaps for a good man someone would even dare to die. But God demonstrates his own love toward us, in that while we were still **sinners**, Christ died for us. Much more then, having now been justified by his blood, we shall be saved from wrath through him. For if when we were **enemies** we were reconciled to God through the death of his Son, much more, having been reconciled, we shall be saved by his life. (Romans 5:6-8, NKJV)*

To be *without strength* means we are weak, feeble or infirmed. We have no power, no ability, no independence, no freedom, no motivation and no ingenuity. We are completely and utterly helpless before the condemnation of our own nature.

To be *ungodly* means we are destitute, needy, lacking or abandoned. It means that we have denied the image of God in which we were created. We are runaways, traitors, deserters, expatriates, Judas Iscariots and haters of God. We are already so far from God that there is little or no resemblance left.

To be *sinners* means we are devoted to sin, especially wicked, or stained with particular vices or crimes. Sinners are not just familiar with sin; they are a *fan of sin*. They are not just a *member* of the "Sinners Club," they are also the *president*, the "chief of sinners" (1 Timothy 1:15). I'm an expert at sinning, an artisan, and a master craftsman, methodical and accomplished.

When Paul completes his description of how awful sin is, he asks: "O wretched man that I am! Who shall deliver me from the body of this death?" (Romans 7:24). He has his answer in the following verse: "I thank God through Jesus Christ our Lord" (Romans 7:25). We're in a mess we can't get out of. We need mercy, not law.

> There is only one sin that is outside the grace of God, and that is the rejection of Jesus Christ, because when we reject Christ, we reject our only lifeline.
>
> **–Troccoli & Brestin**

The Hebrew word for *forgive* is *calach*, which means, "to forgive, to pardon." The verb tense implies that *calach* is a continual action. The blood of Jesus is sufficient to cover sins; past, present, and future – but God is continually pouring forgiveness into our lives. When God forgives, he pardons. He doesn't just wipe the slate clean, he gives us a completely new slate. The sin is completely gone. We are clean once again. Since the heart of *forgiveness* is the idea of *giving*, we know there's no way we can earn it. So God gives freely, and abundantly pours it on our behalf.

God, however, will not circumvent the will of a human being. He designed our will and it is holy to him. He will not *force* anyone to love him. As we might guess, our rejection grieves God deeply. Consider what Jesus said when he wept over Jerusalem:

> *O Jerusalem, Jerusalem, the one who kills the prophets and stones those who are sent to her! How often I wanted to gather your children together, as a hen gathers her chicks under her wings, but you were not willing! See! Your house is left to you desolate; for I say to you, you shall see Me no more till you say, 'Blessed is he who comes in the name of the LORD!' (Matthew 23:37-39)*

God respects us as individuals enough to let us make our own mistakes. He will allow situations to take place in our life in order for us to face our sin, but if we choose to ignore it, he will let us. Kathy Troccoli and Dee Brestin wrote, "There is only one sin that is outside the grace of God, and that is the rejection of Jesus Christ, because when we reject Christ, we reject our only lifeline."[6] If we decide to turn our back on God, he will allow himself to be rejected.

The good news is that *atonement is available.* Redemption for our sin is possible. God is ready to forgive. Only one thing is required: accepting Jesus Christ as Lord and savior over our lives. John 14:6 says, "I am the way, the truth and the life. No one comes to the father except through me. Forgiveness of sin is only accepted when we receive Jesus as our Lord and savior. We must take responsibility for our sins and give ourselves to him completely. The apostle John explains the process very simply in 1 John 1:9.

> *If we confess our sins, he is faithful and just to forgive us our sins, and to cleanse us from all unrighteousness.*

Confession of sin simply means repentance. The word repent in Hebrew is the word *shuv,* and it means 'to change' or 'to turn.' Once an individual hears the message of Jesus Christ and receives him as Lord and Savior, the Holy Spirit will convict that person's heart of

---

[6] Living in Love with Jesus: 74.

his current behavior which influences the person to change his or her present state of being. Repentance is not an emotional state of mind or a feeling of guilt, but rather an acknowledgement of our fall from grace by confessing our sins to our father who is the only one who can forgive us of all of our sins. Once we have acknowledged our sins, we must confess them. Once we have confessed our sins to the father, we must turn away from the sinful behavior. Complete restoration doesn't occur until we turn away from past behaviors, ungodly thoughts and desires.

David, the man after God's own heart (1 Samuel 13:13-14), took the time to describe both his time away from God and his journey back to God in Psalm 51.

1. He proclaimed his helplessness (1-2).

To get out of this sin mess, God is going to have to do the lifting.

Have mercy upon me, O God, according to thy lovingkindness: according unto the multitude of thy tender mercies blot out my transgressions. Wash me thoroughly from mine iniquity, and cleanse me from my sin.

2. He acknowledged his sinfulness (3-4).

When we sin, God suffers the most. It is as though we crucify Christ afresh. To receive forgiveness, we must take ownership of our sins.

For I acknowledge my transgressions: and my sin is ever before me. Against thee, thee only, have I sinned, and done this evil in thy sight: that thou mightest be justified when thou speakest, and be clear when thou judgest.

3. He requested godliness (5-7).

Although we were created in God's image, we can claim none of his righteousness, meaning that we have no way to lift ourselves away from our sinful nature. God must purge us and wash us of our iniquity.

Behold, I was shapen in iniquity; and in sin did my mother conceive me. Behold, thou desirest truth in the inward parts: and in the hidden part thou shalt make me to know wisdom. Purge me with hyssop, and I shall be clean: wash me, and I shall be whiter than snow.

4. He craved joyfulness (8).

The loss of relationship with God is heartbreaking for us and for God. David missed his relationship with God. He longed for God's approval again. He coveted the joy of the Lord.

Make me to hear joy and gladness; that the bones which thou hast broken may rejoice.

5. He prayed for cleanness (9-12).

In the presence of absolute purity, we cannot help but clearly see our utter filthiness. To a certain extent, God ignores aspects of our sinfulness. There are things about us that he simply chooses not to point out when we come to him in confession and repentance, because he is kind. He wants them gone, but he wants us to survive the cleansing as well. He creates a new heart *in* us, replacing our sin with his righteousness in our hearts. Jesus' righteousness works from that point on to clean up everything else.

Hide thy face from my sins, and blot out all mine iniquities. Create in me a clean heart, O God; and renew a right spirit within me. Cast me not away from thy presence; and take not thy holy spirit from me. Restore unto me the joy of thy salvation; and uphold me with thy free spirit.

6. He pledged witness (13-15).

Every forgiven person has the obligation to be viral, to be a righteous contagion, to be a witness and announcer of God's great forgiveness. David permanently links evangelism to forgiveness.

Then will I teach transgressors thy ways; and sinners shall be converted unto thee. Deliver me from bloodguiltiness, O God, thou God of my salvation: and my tongue shall sing aloud of thy righteousness. O Lord, open thou my lips; and my mouth shall shew forth thy praise.

7. He understood righteousness (9-12).

David grasped the notion that, even though he was forgiven, he still was not good enough to be righteous on his own. There was still nothing he could do to earn God's favor or gain God's righteousness. He knew that he must continue to call on God's mercy. In doing so, *everything* he did would delight God and everything he said would reflect God. David's image would be godly as long as he depended on God for his very existence. God, in turn, would do the work of conforming David to reflect his goodness and holiness, transforming him to be an instrument God could use for his glory.

For thou desirest not sacrifice; else would I give it: thou delightest not in burnt offering. The sacrifices of God are a broken spirit: a broken and a contrite heart, O God, thou wilt not despise. Do good in thy good pleasure unto Zion: build thou the walls of Jerusalem. Then shalt thou be pleased with the sacrifices of righteousness, with burnt offering and whole burnt offering: then shall they offer bullocks upon thine altar.

Psalm 19:12-14 does a beautiful job describing the confrontation with our own sin that we must have in order to receive God's atonement:

*Who can understand his **errors**?*

Errors are wrongs committed accidentally in moments of inattention or simple oversight. However, even though they may have been unintentional, they still cause hurt and must be dealt with.

*Cleanse thou me from **secret faults.***

Secret faults are wrongs committed through ignorance or lack of knowledge. While dying on the cross and in excruciating pain both physically and mentally, Jesus prayed for his tormenters in spite of their ignorance:

> *Then said Jesus, "Father, forgive them; for they know not what they do." (Luke 23:34)*

David's cry in Psalm 19:13 was begging God to prevent him from committing presumptuous sins. "Keep back thy servant also from presumptuous sins; let them not have dominion over me: then shall I be upright, and I shall be innocent from the great transgression (Psalm 19:13).

Presumptuous sins are wrongs committed through prideful insolence, such as when the priests in Jerusalem told the Israelites that there was no need to put away their idols. As long as they had the temple. In their opinion, God would never allow Jerusalem to fall into the hands of the Babylonians.[7]

---

[7] Jeremiah 7:9-14- [9]Will ye steal, murder, and commit adultery, and swear falsely, and burn incense unto Baal, and walk after other gods whom ye know not; [10]And come and stand before me in this house, which is called by my name, and say, We are delivered to do all these abominations? [11]Is this house, which is called by my name, become a den of robbers in your eyes? Behold, even I have seen it, saith the LORD. [12]But go ye now unto my place which was in Shiloh, where I set my name at the first, and see what I did to it for the wickedness of my people Israel. [13]And now, because ye have done all these works, saith the LORD, and I spake unto you, rising up early and speaking, but ye heard not; and I called you, but ye answered not; [14]Therefore will I do unto this house, which is called by my name, wherein ye trust, and unto the place which I gave to you and to your fathers, as I have done to Shiloh.

At the end we are left with a beautiful process of atonement. The wanderer has been rescued, the cast-off salvaged and the rebel reconciled:

Let the words of my mouth, and the meditation of my heart, be acceptable in thy sight, O LORD, my strength, and my redeemer. (Psalm 19:14)

God Accepts

There is therefore now no condemnation to those who are in Christ Jesus, who do not walk according to the flesh, but according to the Spirit. (Romans 8:1)

The word for *sin* in 2 Chronicles 7:14 is *chatta'ah*. It refers to both the condition of sin and the punishment for sin. This has great significance for believers. When God forgives, He makes us completely clean. We are no longer a filthy sinner because the *condition* of our sin is gone. Then, God goes a step further: he also removes the *punishment* for our sin. That does not mean that the consequences of our sins are gone. The repercussions of wrong actions and attitudes still have to be dealt with. But there is no guilt, no shame and no condemnation. The sin is *gone* - as far as the east is from the west.[8]

Paul set a very high goal for believers:

Now may the God of peace himself **sanctify** you **completely**; and may your whole **spirit, soul,** and **body** be **preserved** blameless at the coming of our Lord Jesus Christ. He who calls you is faithful, who also will do it. (1 Thessalonians 5:23-24)

Let's examine a few of those words:
- *Sanctify* means to be separate from the profane and dedicated to God; purified.

---

[8] Psalm 103:12

- *Completely* means that something permeates the person through and through; they are "finished" in all respects. Their lives have been consummated in Christ.

- *Spirit* means "breath." In the Bible, it is often a reference to the infilling, or the *making* alive, of a human. It specifies the part of mankind that came from God's image: his personality and character.

- *Soul* means the psyche, the desires, motivations and feelings of a person.

- *Body* means the physical being of a person, that which can be perceived by the five senses.

- *Preserved* means guarded, tended carefully or kept. It has to do with safety and security.

Altogether, Paul's blessing designates that the whole person, body, soul and spirit, is capable of purification by the God of peace. Submitting to God with the body, soul and spirit results in *integration* with him. God saves all parts of us: our nature, our motives and our past, and unites us to his image. Our encounter with his saving grace leaves us perfect and entire, missing nothing (James 1:4).

Once we have experienced his forgiveness, the God of the universe says he is pleased with us. Just as he did with the woman caught in sin, God whispers this promise into our life: "Neither do I condemn you. Go and sin no more" (John 8:1-11). There is no condemnation. We must face the consequences of our actions, but we no longer have to bear the shame or guilt.

. . . and yet we do. We still carry much guilt and shame from our past actions. God no longer condemns us – but we condemn ourselves. This is not God's plan. As a matter of fact, it contradicts God's plan. Troccoli and Brestin write: "Is there a sin in your past that is still causing you guilt? Jesus died to pay for that sin. Don't hold onto it. Give it to Jesus - believe His promises - otherwise you are saying that His death was not sufficient to pay for your sin."[9]

> Is there a sin in your past that is still causing you guilt? Jesus died to pay for that sin. Don't hold on to it. Give it to Jesus - believe his promises - otherwise you are saying that his death was not sufficient to pay for your sin.
>
> **–Troccoli & Brestin**

Before time began, God knew the mistakes we would make. Knowing all this, he still says, "I am especially fond of you."

God Adopts

God's forgiveness cleanses us from sin and puts us in a right relationship with God. We will live in a new identity as His child, his disciple, his friend and his beloved. It is important to remember that Jesus is God's "only begotten Son." (John 3:16) – his only "birth-child." Every other child of God is adopted. Follow Paul as he explores what it means to be God's adopted child.

---

[9] Troccoli and Brestin: 75.

In his letter to the Church in Rome, Paul explains that the only way to preserve our flesh is to be adopted spiritually by God, which gives us joint-inheritance with Christ in all God's good things.

> *For if you live according to the flesh you will die; but if by the Spirit you put to death the deeds of the body, you will live. For as many as are led by the Spirit of God, these are sons of God. For you did not receive the spirit of bondage again to fear, but you received the Spirit of adoption by whom we cry out, "Abba, Father." The Spirit himself bears witness with our spirit that we are children of God, and if children, then heirs—heirs of God and joint heirs with Christ, if indeed we suffer with him, that we may also be glorified together. (Romans 8:13-17)*

Then he explains that all creation shares in this destiny. The cosmos lives in the dysfunctional family of sin, but God plans to save his precious creation out of that mess, along with us, through the saving work of his Son.

> *For the creation was subjected to futility, not willingly, but because of him who subjected it in hope; because the creation itself also will be delivered from the bondage of corruption into the glorious liberty of the children of God. For we know that the whole creation groans and labors with birth pangs together until now. Not only that, but we also who have the firstfruits of the Spirit, even we ourselves groan within ourselves, eagerly waiting for the adoption, the redemption of our body. For we were saved in this hope, but hope that is seen is not hope; for why does one still hope for what he sees? But if we hope for what we do not see, we eagerly wait for it with perseverance. (Romans 8:20-25)*

No one is exempt from the need for God's adoption. Israel, which had always considered itself a child of God, must also go through this process. Paul admits that they have had an advantage, because they have always possessed God's revelation that the adoption was necessary, even though they disregarded it.

For I could wish that I myself were accursed from Christ for my brethren, my countrymen according to the flesh, who are Israelites, to whom pertain the adoption, the glory, the covenants, the giving of the law, the service of God, and the promises; of whom are the fathers and from whom, according to the flesh, Christ came, who is over all, the eternally blessed God. Amen. (Romans 9:3-5)

In his letter to the church in Galatia, Paul points out to the arrogant pseudo-Jews that they have no bragging rights. God wasn't simply adopting children from nice circumstances and cultured backgrounds; he was adopting *slaves*, Jew and Gentile alike. This makes his adoption all the more gracious. This is God's most intimate act for and with fallen humanity.

Now I say that the heir, as long as he is a child, does not differ at all from a slave, though he is master of all, but is under guardians and stewards until the time appointed by the father. Even so we, when we were children, were in bondage under the elements of the world. But when the fullness of the time had come, God sent forth his Son, born of a woman, born under the law, to redeem those who were under the law, that we might receive the adoption as sons. And because you are sons, God has sent forth the Spirit of his Son into your hearts, crying out, "Abba, Father!" Therefore you are no longer a slave but a son, and if a son, then an heir of God through Christ. (Galatians 4:1-7)

Finally, in his letter to the Church at Ephesus, Paul rejoices in the fact that God wasn't playing catch-up when he chose to adopt us. He knew our nature when we were created and he always knew what he would do when humanity fell to sin. This isn't Plan B. Adoption is God's Plan A.

Blessed be the God and Father of our Lord Jesus Christ, who has blessed us with every spiritual blessing in the heavenly places in Christ, just as He chose us in Him before the foundation of the world, that we should be holy and without blame before Him in love, having predestined us to adoption as sons by Jesus Christ to Himself, according to the good pleasure of His will, to the praise of the glory of His grace, by which He made us accepted in the Beloved. (Ephesians 1:3-6)

He cannot love me more. He cannot love me less.

LIVING UNDER THE LAVISH BLESSING OF GOD

What then shall we say to these things? If God is for us, who can be against us? He who did not spare His own Son, but delivered Him up for us all, how shall He not with Him also freely give us all things? Who shall bring a charge against God's elect? It is God who justifies. Who is he who condemns? It is Christ who died, and furthermore is also risen, who is even at the right hand of God, who also makes intercession for us. Who shall separate us from the love of Christ? Shall tribulation, or distress, or persecution, or famine, or nakedness, or peril, or sword? Yet in all these things we are more than conquerors through Him who loved us. For I am persuaded that neither death nor life, nor angels nor principalities nor powers, nor things present nor things to come, nor height nor depth, nor any other created thing, shall be able to separate us from the love of God which is in Christ Jesus our Lord. (Romans 8:31-39)

Although we already read these verses in the last chapter, they are worth taking a second look. There is something interesting contained in these verses, something we may have missed the first time. As we said before, Paul used these verses to remind the Romans that there is nothing that can separate those who trust God from his love; *NOTHING.* None of the things Paul listed have the power to separate us from God. But that's not all that Paul mentioned. Look closer at the questions Paul asked his readers in verses 31-39:

- If God is for us, who can be against us?
- Who will bring a charge against God's elect?

- Who is he who condemns?
- Who will separate us from God?

What is Paul saying? These are rhetorical questions. He is teaching that *there is no one who has the right to condemn or judge God's children except for God himself;* NO ONE. Satan cannot condemn God's children. Other people cannot condemn us and we cannot condemn ourselves. Face it: we cannot even separate ourselves from God's love. We are clean if God says we are clean. We are right if God says we are right. We are forgiven if God says we are forgiven.

What does it really mean to have God forgive? It is much more than we may think. It means we have the acceptance of Almighty God. Let that truth sink in for a moment. God – the Holy, Righteous and Perfect One – accepts us. But there is more. We have God's acceptance because we first have his atonement and his adoption. He sacrificed his Son so that we could become his child. And now that we have received that gift, we can live in full assurance that God is pleased with us.

As with *hearing, knowing* that God forgives and *living* the reality of that truth are two very different things. Living under the lavish blessing of God happens when we start believing God above all others. Whether we feel like it or not, God forgives us. If we have accepted the work that Christ did on the cross for us, to pay our sin debt, and have received

> NO ONE HAS THE RIGHT TO CONDEMN OR JUDGE GOD'S CHILDREN EXCEPT FOR GOD HIMSELF.

it for ourselves and our own sinful condition, then we have been wiped clean and made new. Now we must walk in the reality of that truth. There is no condemnation, no guilt or shame. There is only grace, love and forgiveness.

I WILL FORGIVE THEIR SIN . . .

I HAVE ATONED FOR YOUR SIN. I ACCEPT YOU AS YOU ARE. I HAVE ADOPTED YOU AS MY CHILD.

Your Turn

1. Have you given your life to God by trusting Jesus as your Savior? If so, describe when and how you did that.

    _____

    _____

    _____

    _____

    _____

2. What does it mean to you that God calls you HIS?

    _____

    _____

    _____

    _____

3. How are you representing God? Are you giving him a good reputation? What do people learn about him by watching you?

    _____

    _____

    _____

    _____

    _____

Chapter 3:

Heal Their Land

When God Heals, We Have His *Abundance*.

Whether we admit it or not, at some point we all fall into the trap of believing the worst about God. Although God has given us no reason to doubt his love or his plan, we have likely all said or thought things such as:

> *If I surrender my life to God, he won't let me have any fun.*
> *If I surrender my family to God, he will take them away from me.*
> *If I surrender my dreams to God, he will give me the opposite of what I want.*

Why do we do that? Why do we automatically assume that life will be miserable if it is under God's control? Why do we believe that lie? The truth is that God wants us to have abundance. He doesn't have a ho-hum existence planned for us. No, God has an adventure far beyond anything our human minds can even imagine for ourselves awaiting those who trust him and trust themselves to him. The Bible is full of evidence of this lavish God:

> For I know the thoughts that I think toward you, says the LORD, thoughts of peace and not of evil, to give you a future and a hope. (Jeremiah 29:11)

> But as it is written: "Eye has not seen, nor ear heard, nor have entered into the heart of man the things which God has prepared for those who love Him." (1 Corinthians 2:9)

> Now to Him who is able to do exceedingly abundantly above all that we ask or think, according to the power that works in us, 21 to Him be glory in the church by Christ Jesus to all generations, forever and ever. (Ephesians 3:20-21)

The truth about God is that he wants what is good for us. He has only our best interest at heart. It's true that sometimes what is good for us is not always pleasant. That's why children argue against eating vegetables and teenagers complain about curfews; but God doesn't just want what is *good,* and he doesn't just want what is better; he wants what is *best.* He wants what is *more.* It has often been said: "That which is good is the enemy of that which is best." God wants to blow our minds with his goodness. He wants to thrill us with his power. He wants us to stand amazed in his presence. That is the whole point of his lavish blessing. It is also the point behind the word *heal.*

Why does God heal?

The purpose of miracles was to authenticate Jesus' ministry - to show that he was who he said he was and that he could do what he said he could do. Why did he want to do this? Was it to show how great he was so that he could feel good about himself? No! The purpose was to bring glory to himself...not for his own ego, but to point to the saving power that was available to all who would seek it. Jesus himself said that he did miracles for four basic reasons:

1. To prove he was sent by God (John 5:36, 14:8-11)
2. To establish his authority (Matthew 9:1-6).
3. To fulfill prophecy (Matthew 8:16-17)
4. To cause us to believe (John 20:30-31)

Jesus didn't simply do miracles to show off his power. He performed miracles as an extension of his mercy. Every miracle Jesus performed was accompanied by forgiveness. God will not heal our bodies at the expense of our souls. He will do whatever it takes to draw us into a closer relationship with him.

Jesus commanded nature and exerted his power over demons to show that he is a God who provides and a God who protects. Jesus conquered disease and death to teach more than physical healing. To those who cannot walk, Jesus came to be the Way, to show us how to walk. To those who cannot see, Jesus came to be the Truth, to call us out of darkness into light. To those who are dying, Jesus came to be the Life, to enable us to be truly alive and completely free.

Jesus most often performed miracles of healing. He healed many people, but he did not heal every person he encountered. Remember, Jesus performed miracles as a support for his teaching not to show off his power. So, in his God-wisdom, he chose to heal certain people and not heal others.

Does God still perform miracles today? Yes, he definitely does! His healing powers have not ceased. Jesus is the same yesterday, today and forever.[10] Yet we cannot forget that God cares more about our souls than about our bodies. He cares more about faith than about proof and he cares more about loving us than about impressing us.

What does it mean to be healed?

The Hebrew word for *heal* is *rapha*. It means "to make healthful, to mend, to cure, console; to pardon, restore." It is interesting that this word refers to both *national hurts* and *personal distresses*. When God promised to heal their land, he meant that he would bring restoration both to the entire nation of Israel as well as individual lives.

---

[10] Hebrews 13:8

The Greek word for *heal* is *sozo*. It means "to save or rescue from danger; to make whole or complete." In the original language, the *healing* does not just mean removing a physical illness; it refers to a total restoration of the person. When Jesus healed people, he made them new. By accomplishing more than physical wellness, he proved himself to be Lord over disease and not just a medical practitioner. Jesus healed all kinds of illnesses and impairments.[11] There was no infirmity that he could not handle.

If we look deeper into the meaning of the word *heal*, we find that Jesus' healing goes beyond the physical and touches our innermost being. Jesus is powerful enough to handle any and all physical diseases, but he is also strong enough to conquer our emotional and spiritual sickness too. It's interesting that the infirmities that Jesus healed most often were leprosy, blindness and paralysis. Jesus had a special place in his ministry for those who were being killed by their flesh, those who could not see and those who could not walk. If we think of those same illnesses in spiritual terms, we will see a vital element of Jesus' heart. He came to be the Life, to show us what it means to be truly alive and completely free. He came to be the Truth, to call us out of darkness and into light. He came to be the Way, to teach us how we should walk.

Too many times when we talk about healing, we only think in physical terms, but that is not a complete Biblical definition of healing. God is first and foremost concerned with the healing of our souls. Consider this example from the Scripture:

> Now it happened on a certain day, as he was teaching, that there were Pharisees and teachers of the law sitting by, who had come out of every town of Galilee, Judea, and Jerusalem. And the power

of the Lord was present to heal them. Then behold, men brought on a bed a man who was paralyzed, whom they sought to bring in and lay before him. And when they could not find how they might bring him in, because of the crowd, they went up on the housetop and let him down with his bed through the tiling into the midst before Jesus.

When he saw their faith, he said to him, "Man, your sins are forgiven you." And the scribes and the Pharisees began to reason, saying, "Who is this who speaks blasphemies? Who can forgive sins but God alone?"
But when Jesus perceived their thoughts, he answered and said to them, "Why are you reasoning in your hearts? Which is easier, to say, 'Your sins are forgiven you,' or to say, 'Rise up and walk'? But that you may know that the Son of Man has power on earth to forgive sins"—he said to the man who was paralyzed, "I say to you, arise, take up your bed, and go to your house." Immediately he rose up before them, took up what he had been lying on, and departed to his own house, glorifying God. (Luke 5:17-25)

Luke sets the scene very carefully: Jesus was teaching in someone's house and many Pharisees and teachers of the law were present. These religious leaders had come from all over the nation to hear Jesus speak. So many were crowded into the house that there was no room for anyone to get near Jesus.

After describing the audience, Luke mentions something very significant: "And the power of the Lord was present to heal them." The first question that automatically comes to mind is: Didn't Jesus *always* have power to heal? The answer to that is *yes*...but Luke is making a point here. There are three different Greek words translated *power* in the New Testament:

1. *Ischus* means "ability, force, strength, might."[12]

2. *Dunamis* can mean "(1) strength power, ability; (2) inherent power, power residing in a thing by virtue of its nature, or which a person or thing exerts and puts forth; (3) power for performing miracles; (4) moral power and excellence of soul; (5) the power and influence which belong to riches and wealth; (6) power and resources arising from numbers; (7) power consisting in or resting upon armies, forces, hosts."[13]

3. *Exousia* can mean " (1) power of choice, liberty of doing as one pleases (leave or permission); (2) physical and mental power; (3) the power of authority (influence) and right (privilege) [14]

All three words are needed in understanding the fullness of Jesus' power, because each word offers a glimpse into specific aspects of his power over diseases:

ABIITY
ACCOMPLISHMENT
AUTHORITY

- *Ischus* points to Jesus' *ability*.
- *Dunamis* refers to Jesus' *accomplishment*.
- *Exousia* explains Jesus' *authority*.

Jesus always has *ischus*, the ability to heal. Sometimes he uses that power and turns it into *dunamis,* the intent to heal. Jesus enters every house with the *ability* to heal but he entered that specific house with the *intent* to heal. Interestingly, Jesus later said that he intended to use

---

[12] The New Testament Greek Lexicon,
http://www.studylight.org/lex/grk/view.cgi?number=2479
[13] Ibid., http://www.studylight.org/lex/grk/view.cgi?number=1411
[14] Ibid. http://www.studylight.org/lex/grk/view.cgi?number=1849

his *dunamis* to show his *exousia*: he accomplished something in order to prove his authority.

ADDICTION =
ANYTHING YOU
CAN'T SAY *NO* TO

STRONGHOLD=
ANYTHING YOU
CAN'T GET OUT OF

IDOL =
ANYTHING YOU
CAN'T LET GO OF

LOVER =
ANYTHING THAT
TAKES GOD'S PLACE
IN YOUR LIFE

Jesus entered the house resolved to heal. Who was he there to heal? He was there to heal the Pharisees and the teachers of the law. We soon realize that the lame man was not really the focus; he was the interruption. Jesus intended to heal the religious leaders through his teaching. They were the ones who were spiritually paralyzed that day.

However, the miracle Jesus gave the man was not the one the friends expected. Yes, Jesus healed the man, but only after he *forgave* him. Remember, though this healing and teaching was really for the benefit of the religious leaders. Jesus knew their hearts and their thoughts. He used this man's situation to show his power and love to the others gathered in the house. He healed the man's legs, but his true intent was to change the minds and hearts of the other people.

Of what do we need healing?

God's first step in restoring us is to forgive our sin, but other things keep us from being whole or complete. Many other wounds need to be mended. God also wants to heal us from addictions, strongholds, idols and lovers.

An *addiction* is anything *we can't say "no" to*. It does not have to be something "bad" such as drugs, alcohol or pornography. We can also be addicted to eating, shopping or working.

A *stronghold* is anything *we can't get out of*. It is a trap, or a snare. This term usually makes me think of relationships. Most of us have been in relationships that started out all right but turned unhealthy over time. By the time we realized how unhealthy the relationship was, we were in so deep that we couldn't get out.

An *idol* is anything *we can't let go of*. Like addictions, idols do not have to be "bad." We can make an idol out of many of God's gifts: family, church, job and talents to name a few. God gave us these things as blessings, but sometimes we cherish them to the point of idolatry. We make them more important than God – and we clutch them tightly when he tries to take them away.

A lover is anything that *takes God's place in our life*. Usually they are people although they do not have to be. A lover is an extreme idol. It is not just as important as God is – a lover *is* a god. A lover *replaces* God.

These addictions, strongholds, idols and lovers are things that keep people from experiencing God's abundance. They create blinders in the lives of believers. They are so afraid of losing them that they fight God over them.

How does God bring healing?
The word *rapha* is in the *qal imperfect tense*. The qal tense is *active* – the healing is something God does himself. He does not send an angel or an intercessor to do it. When we are being healed, God himself is actively involved. The imperfect tense means that it is a *process*. Most of the time, healing is not instantaneous, although a miracle-working

God is certainly capable of that. God brings wholeness and completeness to our lives through an ongoing process.

Mark 5:25-34 tells a beautiful story of healing faith:

> *Now a certain woman had a flow of blood for twelve years, and had suffered many things from many physicians. She had spent all that she had and was no better, but rather grew worse. When she heard about Jesus, she came behind him in the crowd and touched his garment. For she said, "If only I may touch his clothes, I shall be made well." Immediately the fountain of her blood was dried up, and she felt in her body that she was healed of the affliction. And Jesus, immediately knowing in himself that power had gone out of him, turned around in the crowd and said, "Who touched my clothes?" But his disciples said to him, "You see the multitude thronging You, and You say, 'Who touched Me?'"*
>
> *And he looked around to see her who had done this thing. But the woman, fearing and trembling, knowing what had happened to her, came and fell down before him and told him the whole truth. And he said to her, "Daughter, your faith has made you well. Go in peace, and be healed of your affliction."*[15]

The woman approached Jesus quietly and in secret. In those days, a person or thing could contract ritual "uncleanness" (or "impurity") in a variety of ways, according to God's instruction: by skin diseases, discharges of bodily fluids, touching something or eating unclean foods. By touching Jesus, she would be breaking God's law and making him unclean. She could not and would not make herself known - both for her sake and for his. However, her desperation made her do *something*. Mark tells us that she "suffered from many physicians." She had spent all of her money going to various doctors in an attempt to find a cure. Not only did she not find a cure, but also all of their medications and procedures actually made her worse. She

---

[15] NKJV

had one option left. It was a long shot, and a possibly dangerous act if she was discovered, but she had to try.

Some commentators wondered if the woman had a superstitious belief about Jesus' clothing. There are no other references to anyone touching Jesus' clothes to be made well. However, there are references to people simply touching Jesus. There are also stories of people being healed from a distance. Whatever her motivation, she knew in her heart that Jesus was so powerful that even a touch of his clothing might be enough.

Jesus later commended her for her faith, but there was also an element of humility in her actions. The woman touched the hem of his robe. In order to do that, she must have been kneeling, possibly even crawling through the crowd to get closer to him. Whether this is humility or humiliation, the woman demonstrated that she did not consider herself worthy of a miracle. Perhaps that is why Jesus gave her one anyway.

But there is much more significance to this woman touching the hem of Jesus' garment than simply a humble attitude. In ancient Israel, men wore four-cornered outer tunics with tassels or *tzitziyot*, tied at the bottom to the four corners. These tassels were to remind each Jewish man of his responsibility to fulfill God's commandments. In fact, these tassels were tied into 613 knots to constantly remind them of the 613 laws of Moses. They came to be known as a constant reminder to walk according to God's laws. Wearing these tassels would be comparable to wearing a large Bible on a rope around our necks. They represented the authority of God.

Tzitziyot would have been hanging on the four corners of Jesus' garment, in full view of everyone, including the woman

When the woman touched Jesus, she knew she was touching

something that represented the Word of God, which is always the place where we can find healing for all the needs in our life. Second, she was acknowledging the authority if Jesus.

She was immediately healed and Jesus felt power leave him. Because this is the only time he says anything like that during a healing, no one knows for certain what he meant. However, the important point here is that her touch did not make Jesus unclean; instead, his touch made her whole.

The next part of this story seems rude at first. Jesus knew she had been healed, and the woman knew that she had been healed. Why did he call her out of the crowd?

First, he did it for the crowd's sake. The woman's infirmity was private in nature, so Jesus offered proof of her healing. Second, he did it for the man with whom Jesus was walking with and whose house they were on their way to, to give him an example of faith in action. And finally, he did it for the woman. She needed to know that her physical healing was true. Although she knew it at the moment, doubt would eventually plague her. She also needed to know that she did not steal a blessing. Jesus freely and willingly healed her.

The beautiful part of this story is that her healing did not stop with her flow of blood. No, by calling her out of the crowd, Jesus restored her emotionally and spiritually. He gave her back a place in the society, and he also gave her a place in his family when he called her "daughter." The apostle Mark says it so beautifully when he tells us that Jesus *looked* for her. He did this on purpose. He looked for her. He spoke to her. He loved her. And He wanted her to know it. It is a beautiful picture of how Jesus looks for us, loves us, and wants us to know it and be healed.

Jesus' healing miracles were always:

- *Immediate.* The word *immediately* appears 53 times in the King James Translation of the Gospels and the Book of Acts. Half of those uses (26) appear in connection with a miraculous act of Christ or his apostles. Of those, 23 describe the manner of Christ's healing.[16]

- *Complete.* There were no residual effects. Jesus does nothing halfway. Remember James 1, where James describes the perfecting work of turmoil in our lives:

  My brethren, count it all joy when you fall into various trials, knowing that the testing of your faith produces patience. But let patience have its perfect work, that you may be perfect and complete, lacking nothing.[17]

- *Thorough.* There is no physical healing without emotional and spiritual healing. Remember Paul's goal for the Thessalonian believers:

  Now may the God of peace Himself **sanctify** you **completely**; and may your whole **spirit, soul,** and **body** be **preserved** blameless at the coming of our Lord Jesus Christ. He who calls you is faithful, who also will do it.[18]

Let's return to the woman with the issue of blood to see these truths clearly. She was healed immediately. She was healed completely. She was healed thoroughly. By calling her out, Jesus was restoring her emotional and spiritual health. He gave her a place in the society and a place in his family.

---

[16] *Matthew 8:3; 14:31; 20:34; Mark 1:31, 42; 2:8, 12; 5:2, 30; 10:52; Luke 1:64; 4:39; 5:13, 25; 8:44, 47; 13:13; 18:43; John 5:9; Acts 3:7; 9:18, 34; 13:11.*
[17] *James 1:2-4, NKJV*
[18] *1 Thessalonians 5:23-24*

But, then Jesus said something odd. In verse 34, He announces: "Daughter, your faith has made you well. Go in peace, and be healed of your affliction."[19] Why would He say that? Wasn't she already healed? Why would He tell her to go and be healed?

The word translated *well* in that verse is the Greek word *sozo*. It means "to be safe; to be rescued from danger or suffering." The word translated *healed* is *hygies*, which means, "to be sound, whole, restored." Jesus is clearly referring to two different kinds of healing: *rescue* and *restoration*.

The truly interesting part of verse 34, though, is the verb tense. When Jesus said, "Your faith has made you well," he was using the *perfect tense*. That tense describes an action that is viewed as having been completed in the past, once and for all, not needing to be repeated. However, when Jesus said, "Be healed," he was using the *imperative* tense, which meant a command requiring obedience.

Read the verse in the *Amplified Bible* to get a better sense of what Jesus was saying to her:

> *And he said to her, "Daughter, your faith (your trust and confidence in Me, springing from faith in God) has restored you to health. Go in (into) peace and be continually healed and freed from your [distressing bodily] disease."*

So, what is the point? Jesus *sozoed* the woman. She had been rescued from her suffering once and for all, never to return, but her *hygies* was optional. She could choose to obey Jesus and experience restoration, or she could continue to live like a sick person. That seems odd when we think about it: Why would a person who no longer has cancer continue taking chemotherapy? Why would a freed prisoner go back to a jail cell? It doesn't make any sense, yet Christians do it all the

---

19 Mark 5:34 NKJV

time. In sociology, this is known as *recidivism*. It is defined as "a tendency to relapse into a previous condition or mode of behavior; *especially*: relapse into criminal behavior."[20] Our basic instinct is to go back to destructive patterns of behavior.

As in 2 Peter 2:22 where we read, "But it is happened unto them according to the true proverb, the dog is turned to his own vomit again; and the sow that was washed to her wallowing in the mire," we too have a hard time living like we are forgiven. We have a hard time acting well. It's the only thing we know and we miss it. It is one of those *addictions* we have a hard time saying no to. It is one of those *idols* we can't let go of. It is one of those *strongholds* we can't escape, *a lover* that takes God's place in our lives. Jesus has rescued us from every emotional and spiritual sickness, and he greatly desires for us to live in restoration. But the choice is ours.

What is our part in the healing process?
The cliché but true statement is that the first step toward healing is to admit that we need healing. This can be a hard step to take in our culture. Just as we saw with asking for forgiveness, asking for healing means admitting that we can't help ourselves. We need someone else to step in and save the day. Too many times, this is an admission that many people do not like to make. But here's the thing: we are broken whether we like to admit it or not. We are broken in a way that we cannot fix. The first thing we need to do is admit to God that we need him to heal us.

[20] Merriam-Webster Online Dictionary, http://www.merriam-webster.com/dictionary/recidivism.

John chapter 5 presents Jesus at the Temple celebrating one of the Jewish feasts, when he encountered a crippled man. While thousands walked by this man as if he was invisible, Jesus took notice of him. While no one else cared what the man had endured, Jesus was well aware, and he went into action.

Jesus' question at first seems odd. It might even come across as rude or cruel. He asked the man, "Do you want to be well?"[21] Did he really have to ask a man who had been lame for 38 years if he wanted to be better? Apparently, yes, He did. Jesus used the question to reveal the man's heart - his desire to be free - not because Jesus didn't know the answer, but because the man himself needed to know.

Scotty Smith explains: "Healing has its consequences. If healed, this invalid would have to learn a whole new way of living. Cure can be scary. Freedom can be thrilling, but can also be intimidating and threatening.[22]"

> Healing has its consequences. If healed, this invalid would have to learn a whole new way of living. Cure can be scary. Freedom can be thrilling, but can also be intimidating and threatening.
>
> –Scotty Smith

Unlike the other lame man, this man did not have friends to help him. For 38 years, he had been completely dependent on other people but he was running out of people who cared enough to help him. One can hear the desperation and loneliness in his voice when he explains his situation to Jesus. "I have no one . . . "

---

[21] John 9:6
[22] Objects of His Affection

The lame man saw the pool as his only hope. But God himself was standing in front of him with a different plan. John Calvin said, "The sick man does what we all do. He limits God's help to his own ideas and does not dare promise himself more than he conceives in his mind." Oh, but our God is the One who delights in doing more than we can hope or imagine[23]- and he was about to do more for this man!"

There are so many Christians still sitting around like lame men. They are focusing on the problems at hand instead of looking up to God the healer of life. Generally, there are five basic attitudes that keep us paralyzed:

> The sick man does what we all do. He limits God's help to his own ideas and does not dare promise himself more than he conceives in his mind.
>
> John Calvin

1. *I don't need God;* i.e., pride. We often have an inordinate need for independence. This can be a big barrier between us and God's healing.

2. *I don't want God;* i.e., lust. Since we have free will, we behave as though we need to exercise it all the time. We choose other things. Our lives are bound up in personal choice, sometimes to the expense of everything else.

3. *I don't deserve God;* i.e., shame. The root of "works" salvation is the idea that God's favor must be earned. But that simply can't be done. Salvation is a gift of grace; it always has been, and it always will be.

---

[23] Ephesians 3:20

4. *I don't trust God;* i.e., unbelief. The first sin was a result of doubting God's goodness.[24] It is quite literally Satan's oldest trick. It is probably his most effective method of tempting believers.

5. *God doesn't care;* i.e., hopelessness. This was Job's fear. Job didn't sin in his tribulation, as his whole family and all of his wealth was taken from him. But he began to doubt whether God had any interest in him, or if he was just a remote essence with no concern for his creation.

What is paralyzing us? What is keeping us from walking with God, from moving forward? No healing is difficult for Jesus because he already did the hard work on the cross. He did his part. Do we want to be well? Are we willing to deal with a little discomfort in exchange for a different way of living? Are we willing to trust God to do something more, instead of limiting him to what we can see or imagine? Are we willing to get up and walk?

Why would we let God heal us even if the healing process is painful?

There's good news and there's bad news when we allow God to begin the healing process. The good news is that God will do whatever it takes to get his people back to living abundantly. He will not stop until we are healed and he won't back down if the process gets difficult. In God's eyes, healing is worth any amount of pain. Make no mistake, healing can be painful. Before healing comes brokenness. God allowed Peter to be sifted.[25] God wrestled with Jacob.[26] God sent Gomer into the wilderness.[27] He desires for us to

---

[24] Genesis 3:1-7
[25] Luke 22:31-32
[26] Genesis 32:22-30
[27] Hosea 2

be restored as well, and will allow us to be broken when necessary to heal us too.

According to Beth Moore, "If you ask him to make himself so real to you through his word and lavish you with his love, you will enjoy God even when you don't enjoy the confrontation." That is the point of healing. Through the process we discover that knowing God is what abundant living is all about. We eventually reach the place Paul came to when he said:

> I count all things loss for the excellence of the knowledge of Christ Jesus my Lord, for whom I have suffered the loss of all things, and count them as rubbish, that I may gain Christ and be found in him, not having my own righteousness, which is from the law, but that which is through faith in Christ, the righteousness which is from God by faith; that I may know him...[28]

> If you ask him to make himself so real to you through his word and lavish you with his love, you will enjoy God even when you don't enjoy the confrontation.
>
> –Beth Moore

One day Jesus and His disciples encountered a blind man. Jesus didn't choose this man to mess up his life, but to make a point. It was commonly believed that a physical infirmity was punishment for sin, hence the question, "Who sinned?"[29] Jesus' answer is so captivating: "No one sinned. This was allowed so that the glory of God should be revealed in him."[30] Our nature is to get rid of our infirmities. But God says, "I gave you that so that my glory could be revealed in you."

---

[28] Philippians 3:8-10
[29] John 9:2
[30] John 9:3

What does abundant living look like?

> Therefore I also, after I heard of your faith in the Lord Jesus and your love for all the saints, do not cease to give thanks for you, making mention of you in my prayers: that the God of our Lord Jesus Christ, the Father of glory, may give to you the spirit of wisdom and revelation in the knowledge of Him, the eyes of your understanding being enlightened; that you may know what is the hope of His calling, what are the riches of the glory of His inheritance in the saints, and what is the exceeding greatness of His power toward us who believe, according to the working of His mighty power which He worked in Christ when He raised Him from the dead and seated Him at His right hand in the heavenly places, far above all principality and power and might and dominion, and every name that is named, not only in this age but also in that which is to come. (Ephesians 1:15-21)

When we live under the lavish blessing of God, he makes us stand firm, free and full.

God Makes Us Stand Firm

The old hymn says:

> My hope is built on nothing less than Jesus' blood and righteousness.
> I dare not trust the sweetest frame, but wholly lean on Jesus' Name.
> On Christ, the Solid Rock I stand- all other ground is sinking sand.[31]

GOD MAKES US STAND FIRM, FREE, & FULL

The firmness Christ provides is found in his *confidence* and what he has made of us.

Moses had lead Israel out of Egypt and throughout their 40-year times of wandering in the wilderness. When he dies, God charged

---

[31] Edward Mote

Joshua with leading Israel into the land promised to the nation centuries earlier through Abraham. Joshua was intimidated with the huge task of taking Moses' place as Israel's leader, but none-the-less, God encouraged him with these instructions:

> *No man shall be able to stand before you all the days of your life; as I was with Moses, so I will be with you. I will not leave you nor forsake you.* **Be strong and of good courage,** *for to this people you shall divide as an inheritance the land which I swore to their fathers to give them. Only* **be strong and very courageous,** *that you may observe to do according to all the law which Moses my servant commanded you; do not turn from it to the right hand or to the left, that you may prosper wherever you go. This Book of the Law shall not depart from your mouth, but you shall meditate in it day and night, that you may observe to do according to all that is written in it. For then you will make your way prosperous, and then you will have good success. Have I not commanded you?* **Be strong and of good courage;** *do not be afraid, nor be dismayed, for the LORD your God is with you wherever you go." (Joshua 1:5-9, NKJV)*

Notice those comprehensive instructions God gave Joshua:

- I am with you, so be strong and courageous (5-6).
- You have my Word, so be strong and courageous (7-8).
- I am the One giving you orders, so be strong and courageous (9)

It is important to note that God is not interested in *getting by*. He is interested in *victory*. John more or less repeated God's instructions as reassurance to the Ephesian believers:

> *For this is the love of God, that we keep his commandments. And his commandments are not burdensome. For whatever is born of God overcomes the world. And this is the victory that has overcome the world—our faith. Who is he who overcomes the world, but he who believes that Jesus is the Son of God? (1 John 5:3-5, NKJV)*

God Makes Us Stand Free

God has no interest in people who carry their old sins around with them, like Jacob Marley, the grumpy old scrooge in *A Christmas Carol*. He is interested in *freedom* from guilt. Taking responsibility is necessary, but *guilt* and responsibility are not synonymous. Author Beth Moore writes: "God never sheds light on our weaknesses or shortcomings for the sake of condemnation. God makes us aware of hindrances so he can set us free."[32]

Jesus was adamant about the believer's freedom: "If the Son therefore shall make you free, ye shall be free indeed (John 8:36). Paul went to great lengths to describe this freedom:

> *There is therefore now no condemnation to them which are in Christ Jesus, who walk not after the flesh, but after the Spirit. For the law of the Spirit of life in Christ Jesus hath made me free from the law of sin and death. For what the law could not do, in that it was weak through the flesh, God sending his own Son in the likeness of sinful flesh, and for sin, condemned sin in the flesh: That the righteousness of the law might be fulfilled in us, who walk not after the flesh, but after the Spirit. (Romans 8:1-4)*

Perhaps we have been taught that we must keep paying for our past sins but you will find no support for that in the New Testament. To Jesus, *free* means *completely free*. The debt of our sins has been paid in full.

God Makes Us Stand Full

There is nothing worse than a Christian "poor-mouth" someone who always concentrates on the *problems* instead of the *plenty*. What did Jesus say about the kind of existence we are to have once we have accepted him as Lord and Savior? "I am come that they might have life, and that they might have it more *abundantly*" (John 10:10). Take a

---

[32]Breaking Free: 37.

look at all the words Paul uses to describe God's actions on the believer's behalf:

*For this cause I bow my knees unto the Father of our Lord Jesus Christ, of whom **the whole family in heaven and earth** is named, that he would grant you, according to **the riches of his glory**, to be **strengthened with might** by his Spirit in the inner man; that **Christ may dwell in your hearts by faith;** that ye, being **rooted and grounded in love**, may be able to **comprehend with all saints** what is the **breadth**, and **length**, and **depth**, and **height;** and to know the love of Christ, which **passeth knowledge**, that ye might be **filled with all the fulness of God**. Now unto him that is able to do **exceeding abundantly above all that we ask or think**, according to the **power** that worketh in us, unto him be **glory** in the church by Christ Jesus throughout **all ages, world without end**. Amen. (Ephesians 3:14-21)*

Isn't that amazing? It appears that God is ready to gush all over us with his love and power and blessings. We can certainly say *amen* to this praise song:

This is my prayer in the desert, and all that's within me is dry.
This is my prayer in the fire, in weakness or trial or pain.
This is my prayer in the battle, and triumph is still on its way.
This is my prayer in the harvest, when favor and providence flow . . .
All of my life, in every season, you are still God. I have a reason to sing.[33]

---

[33] Hillsong, Desert Song

Living Under the Lavish Blessing of God

But Paul isn't finished describing God's blessings. Here he describes the perspective we must have if we are to live under God's abundance:

Our suffering is temporary, but God's glory is eternal.

> I consider that the sufferings of this present time are not worthy to be compared with the glory which shall be revealed in us (Romans 8:18)

In one of Chaim Potok's books, an old rabbi looks at his family turmoil, and prays, "Master of the Universe, what are you up to?"[34] We can say with confidence God is up to something! Satan is the one who confuses. *God is the One Who* reveals. *Carl Henry described divine revelation in terms of God's acts: he is the God who* stoops, speaks *and* shows.[35] *The solution for Job's discouragement was getting a taste of the eternal. We are living the* eternal life. *We have more than a taste. We are* in it.

When our circumstances reflect havoc and chaos, God is the master strategist.

> We know that all things work together for good to those who love God, to those who are the called according to his purpose. For whom he foreknew, he also predestined to be conformed to the image of his Son, that he might be the firstborn among many brethren. Moreover whom he predestined, these he also called; whom he called, these he also justified; and whom he justified, these he also glorified. (Romans 8:28-30)

The universe is not out of control. The very small part of the world we see is confusing, to say the least, but God plays the hand he has dealt himself and wins

---

[34] My Name is Asher Lev.
[35] God, Revelation, and Authority.

every time. Think of our lives as though it were a cake but concentrate on the ingredients, not the sugary frosting. Suppose we are making a cake from scratch. Few cake ingredients are appetizing on their own. Try eating a couple of tablespoons of cocoa. Or, how about a cup of shortening, with a little baking powder garnish? Some people like raw eggs, but they run the risk of salmonella. What if we only include the ingredients that only taste good on their own? We'll have a bowl of sugar. Or, what if we choose not to bake the cake, because we are afraid of reaching into a hot oven to get it out? Maybe we'd just like to eat the cake batter once it's all mixed up together. That might be tasty, but it can also make us pretty sick. It's the heat that changes the varied ingredients into something appetizing. Soon the house is filled with warm, enticing smells, and we usually don't even want to wait for the icing- just give us a piece of warm cake with some powdered sugar dusting!

Paul tells us that there are ingredients to our life (conflict, challenge, heartache, disappointment, illness, etc.), and there is heat (the process of everything "working together") by which those things turn into something that glorifies God and sanctifies us.

Life is moving in every direction but God will not let circumstances stop his love.

What then shall we say to these things? If God is for us, who can be against us? He who did not spare his own Son, but delivered him up for us all, how shall he not with him also freely give us all things? Who shall bring a charge against God's elect? It is God who justifies. Who is he who condemns? It is Christ who died, and furthermore is also risen, who is even at the right hand of God, who also makes intercession for us. Who shall separate us from the love of Christ? Shall tribulation, or distress, or persecution, or famine, or nakedness, or peril, or sword? Yet in all these things we are more than conquerors through him who loved us. For I am persuaded that neither death nor life, nor angels nor principalities nor powers, nor things present nor things to come, nor height nor depth, nor any other created thing, shall be able to separate us from the love of God which is in Christ Jesus our Lord. (Romans 8:31-39)

In verses 31-39, Paul informed the Romans that nothing and no one could possibly separate them from God's presence and love. Nothing…no one. But Paul also made this promise: once we stand in the full realization that we have God's attention and acceptance, then we will also see that we are "more than a conqueror" through Jesus. <u>We are more</u> than a conqueror. We won't just survive by the skin of our teeth. We won't just *barely* make it. We can stand firm. We can stand free. We can stand full.

What is Paul saying? No difficulty we are going through can be compared to the glory that God has in store for us. He was teaching them that God may allow any number of bad things to come into their lives, but that God would only allow the things that would work for their good. And what good is God working toward? He wants to conform his children to the image of his Son.

What does it really mean to have God heal us? It is so much more than we may think. It means we have the abundance of Almighty God. Let that truth sink in for a moment. God – the Holy, Righteous, and Perfect One – heals us. But he doesn't stop there.

As with hearing and forgiving, knowing the fact that God heals us and living the reality of that truth are two very different things.

I WILL HEAL THEIR LAND…

I MAKE YOU STAND FIRM. I MAKE YOU STAND FREE. I MAKE YOU STAND FULL.

YOUR TURN

1. What area in your life needs healing?

_____

_____

_____

_____

_____

2. Is there a situation in your life that has paralyzed you?

_____

_____

_____

_____

3. What does it mean to live under God's lavish blessing?

_____

_____

_____

_____

Chapter 4:

Called By My Name

When We Belong To God, We Honor God's Name.

I will walk among you and be your God, and you shall be my people. (Leviticus 26:12)

God gives us the option of coming back to him on his terms – and he listed four simple things he expects when we return:
1.   We must humble ourselves.
2.   We must pray.
3.   We must seek his face.
4.   We must turn from our wicked ways.

However, there is one detail that must be dealt with before we address those terms: these expectations only apply to certain people. *"If **My** people who are called by **My** name..."* God does not give a WHEN . . . IF . . . THEN promise to just anyone. The promise only applies to his people. If that does not seem fair, then keep reading. God also promises throughout the Bible that anyone can become one of his people. So, in reality, the 2 Chronicles 7:14 promise does apply to everyone – but it only applies after we have made the choice to belong to God.

If My People

What does it mean to be the people of God? The Hebrew word for *people* is *am*. It can be translated as *people, nation, countrymen* or *kinsmen*. The Hebrew word implies a close relationship. We become God's countrymen when we become citizens of heaven. We are his kinsmen when we are members of his family.

How does a person become a citizen of heaven or a member of God's family? We claim both roles by surrendering our lives to Jesus Christ and by receiving Jesus as our personal Lord and Savior. At some point in life, every person realizes that they are separated from God and can do nothing to fix the broken relationship. Jesus came to do for us what we cannot do for ourselves. He lived a perfect life, died as a perfect sacrifice, and then raised himself completely (or perfectly) from the dead to prove that he, and he alone, had power over death, hell and the grave. When we acknowledge his sacrifice and accept his gift, then we are adopted into God's family. We become God's people.

But there is more to this picture than just a relationship. Notice that God calls us "my people." We are not just *people*; we are *his* people, *his* possessions, *and his* treasures. We belong to him. The moment we choose to follow him, God puts his seal of ownership on us, much like a rancher puts his brand on his cattle to show ownership. If a steer with a certain rancher's brand wanders off or somehow gets mixed in with cattle belonging to another rancher, it soon becomes apparent to everyone that this particular steer belongs to another. Since we belong to God, he is obligated to provide for us and protect us. He has compelled himself to love and care for us. He has to do it. Anything less would be a denial of his own nature (2 Timothy 2:13). All he asks in return is that we love him. He does not want us to follow him out of guilt or obligation. He wants trust. He wants affection. God wants intimacy from his people. We are his – and he is ours.

Who Are Called By My Name

God not only claims us as *his* people, but he *calls* us by his name. The Hebrew word for *called* is *qara*. It means, "to call out, invite, appoint; call and commission; call and endow." Notice the variety of meanings, and yet each one represents what God does for us. He calls out to us, begging us to notice him. He invites us into relationship with him. Then he appoints us for a purpose. When he calls us, he also commissions us (gives us a job to do) and endows us (gives us the ability and the authority to do his will).

This verse would be better translated, "If my people whom I called by my name ..." since the verb is in the *passive perfect tense*. The passive tense shows that we did nothing to earn or create our calling. God did all the work. He is both the author and finisher of our faith (Hebrews 12:3). Let that be a great comfort. We did nothing to earn our place in God's kingdom. His lavish love and unending grace did what was necessary for us to know him. Since we did nothing to earn our place, we can do nothing to lose it.

The *perfect tense* implies a *completed action*. Not only did he do all the work, he did it once and for all. There is nothing else that we need, for he has already supplied it all. We were called, commissioned and endowed the moment we said "yes" to Jesus.

What could be better than that? God called each of us by his *Name*. The word *name* is the Hebrew word *shem*, which means "name, reputation, fame, glory." In ancient Biblical Hebrew culture, a person's name was very important; it was not only used for identifying a person, but also for understanding a person's character.

A person's name defined a person, and were often used to express the nature and function of a person. For example, Abraham was the "father of many nations." Aaron was the "exalted one." Ruth meant "friend." Names were also used to indicate a person's purpose in the world, and the greatest example of this type of naming is Jesus.

> *But after he had considered this, an angel of the Lord appeared to him in a dream and said, "Joseph son of David, do not be afraid to take Mary home as your wife, because what is conceived in her is from the Holy Spirit. She will give birth to a son, and you are to give him the name Jesus, because he will save his people from their sins. (Matthew 1:20-21)*

...because he will save his people from their sins. The name "Jesus" literally means, "The Lord saves." Jesus' primary purpose for existing was to save people from their sins.

It was very common for people to change names or to have more than one name as their lives changed and their personalities grew. Names often revealed character, but they also revealed relationship. A Hebrew name connected that person to their father. Biblical names were sometimes used to secure the solidarity of family ties. An example of this is found in Luke 1:59 when John the Baptist was nearly given the name of his father. The son's name was to indicate that he was like his father, and carried his father's identity. The Hebrews firmly believed in the power of a name and they carried that belief into their encounters with God.

If we have read the book of Genesis, we might recognize *Shem* as one of Noah's sons. Specifically, Shem was the son who started the lineage that led to Abraham and the Israelites. Shortly after Noah and his family survived the Flood, mankind decided to build a tower that reached to heaven (Genesis 11). Actually, what the people wanted was to *make a name for themselves.* They figured they could unite together and create a force that no one could conquer, not even God.

Of course, God showed them the truth by creating different languages to confuse their work. But, the point is not that God was stronger than they were; that fact is not surprising at all. The point is that God was bothered by their plan. His heart was to have a people known by *his* name, not a people who made a name for themselves. So, he chose the descendants of Shem, a people with no name, who could carry his name.

It is not just God's name that we carry. We take on his reputation and his character. Just as a woman takes on her husband's name when she gets married, so we take on God's name when we become part of his family. Our name is forever connected to his name. We are "branded" with his brand. We carry our father's identity and image. Our actions and words now reflect him. People who do not know God learn about him by watching us. That can be both an encouraging and a frightening thought. Just think about it: God trusts *each of us* with his name.

And what is God's name? What reputation or image are we supposed to represent? In the Bible, God is known by three basic names: *Yehovah/Jehovah, Elohim* and *Adonai.* In English Bibles, *Jehovah* or *Yahweh* is written as LORD. It comes from the Hebrew verb "to be" and is God's name for himself – the one he told Moses to use in Exodus 3:14. In fact, a tradition evolved within Judaism to never speak the name of God out of reverence for, and fear of their God. It is God's covenant name and points us to his promises.

In Genesis 1:26, God refers to himself as *Us.* This is the Hebrew name *Elohim,* the plural form of *El,* the supreme being. It is most often translated into the English word *God.* This name points to God's plurality – his triune nature. God the Father, Son and Holy Ghost.

The Hebrew name David used in Psalm 39:7 is *Adonai*. *Adonai* translates to *Lord*, and is used over 300 times in the Old Testament. Notice that both *Yehovah* and *Adonai* are translated *Lord*. Although they are translated to the same word they should be understood differently. The term *Lord* is often misunderstood because it is not a term that we use often in our society. In the Bible, the word can have two different meanings: *absolute sovereignty* or *master/owner*. Either way we translate it, this name points to God's power.

These three names for God give us great insight into his character. He is a God of promises, a God of plurality and a God of power. He is the Supreme Being, the great *I AM*, the *Lord*. Every Hebrew knew God by these names, but it was also common for them to change or add to God's name to reflect a personal connection with him.

Hagar (see Genesis 16:7-13) was an Egyptian slave girl. She belonged to a Hebrew woman named Sarai who treated her badly, causing Hagar to run away. As Hagar was fleeing through the wilderness, God (also called the Angel of the Lord in this passage) appeared to her and spoke with her. Can you imagine what it was like for this woman, this Egyptian slave, to have a one-on-one encounter with the God of Israel? Can you fathom what it meant to her when she realized that the God of the universe took notice of her, a nobody? As a result, she gave him a name: *El-Roi– the God Who Sees.*

People today still use God's various names. I like to be very specific in my prayer time by choosing the name of God that best suits my needs or my reason for coming to him. When I come with a physical need, he is my *Yehovah-Yirah*, the *Lord will Provide*. When someone I love is sick, he is my *Yehovah-Rophe*, the *Lord Who Heals*. When I just need to feel loved, he is the *Lover of my soul* – but when I need answers, he is *Adonai*, the *Almighty Lord*.

Below is a list of Hebrew words that will help you know God by name. Use these names in worship, prayer and quiet times with God, and reflect on these attributes and qualities of God as you serve him and other people.

NAM	MEANING	BIBLE REFERENCES	IMPLICATIONS
El Elyon	Most High God	Genesis 14:20; Psalm 9:2	Stresses God's strength, sovereignty and supremacy
El Olam	Everlasting God	Genesis 16:13	Emphasizes God's unchangeableness and is connected with his inexhaustibleness
El Shaddai	God Almighty	Genesis 17:1; 28:3; 35:11 Exodus 6:31; Psalm 91:1-2	Portrays the Almighty One who corrects and chastens
Yehovah-Yireh	Lord who Provides	Genesis 22:14	Stresses God's provision for his people
Yehovah-Nissi	Lord our Banner	Exodus 17:15	Stresses that God is our rallying point and our means of victory; the one who fights for his people
Yehovah-Shalom	Lord our Peace	Judges 6:24	Points to the Lord as the means of our peace and rest
Yehovah-Shammah	Lord who is There	Ezekiel 48:35	Portrays the Lord's personal presence
Yehovah-Tsidkenu	Lord our Righteousness	Jeremiah 23:5-6	Portrays the Lord as the means of our righteousness
Yehovah Sabbaoth	Lord of Hosts	1 Samuel 1:3; 17:45	Portrays the Lord as commander of the armies of heaven
Yehovah Maccaddeshcem	Lord our Sanctifier	Exodus 31:13	Portrays the Lord as our means of sanctification or as the one who sets believers apart for his purposes
Yehovah Roi	Lord my Shepherd	Psalm 23:1	Portrays the Lord as The Shepherd who cares for his people as a shepherd cares for the sheep of his pasture

The New Testament also uses specific words for God:

NAME	MEANING	BIBLE REFERENCES	IMPLICATIONS
Theos	God	John 1:1, 18; 20:28; 1 John 5:20; Tit. 2:13; Rom. 9:5; Heb. 1:8; 2 Pet. 1:1.	Greek: Primary name for God used in the New Testament. This name is used of Christ as God
Kurios	Lord	Mathew 8:6; John 20:28; Acts 2:36; Romans 10:9; Philippians 2:11	Greek: Stresses authority and supremacy it is used mostly as the equivalent of Yahweh of the Old Testament. It too is used of Jesus Christ meaning (1) Rabbi or Sir; (2) God or Deity
Despotes	Master	Luke 2:29; Acts 4:24; Revelation 6:10; 2 Peter 2:1; Jude 4	Greek: Carries the idea of ownership while kurios stressed supreme authority
Abba	Father	Matthew. 7:11; James 1:17; Hebrews 12:5-11; John 15:16; 16:23; Ephesians 2:18; 3:15; 1 Thessalonians 3:11	Aramaic: A distinctive New Testament revelation is that through faith in Christ, God becomes our personal Father. Father is used of God in the Old Testament only 15 times while it is used of God 245 times in the New Testament. As a name of God, it stresses God's loving care, provision, discipline, and the way we are to address God in prayer

The Lord wants us to know the I AM:

I AM the creator of all the heavens and the earth and all life and matter.

I AM God Almighty.

I AM eternal, all-knowing, ever present, all-wise, righteous, and holy.

I AM sovereign and in control over all.

I AM the judge of all the earth and God of wrath concerning sin.

I AM a jealous God about my very own people.

I AM a God of grace.

I AM the God of mercy and love and compassion and forgiveness.

I AM God and Father of the Lord Jesus Christ.

I AM God of the cross and the resurrection.

YOUR TURN

1. What does it mean to be called by God?

    _____

    _____

    _____

    _____

    _____

2. What has God called you to do?

    _____

    _____

    _____

    _____

    _____

3. What other names can you think of for God?

    _____

    _____

    _____

    _____

    _____

Chapter 5:

Humble Themselves

When We Humble Ourselves, We Show God's Glory.

Humble yourselves in the sight of the Lord, and he will lift you up. (1 Peter 4:10)

Humility is not a quality that is appreciated in Western civilization. We teach even the smallest children to have pride in themselves. *Meekness* is considered a weakness and *submission* a dirty word, and we honor those people who display arrogant confidence.

Is it any wonder that we hate being humble? Just look at these definitions of the word:

HUMBLE (adjective)	having a feeling of insignificance or inferiority; low in rank, importance, status or quality; plain; common, poor
HUMBLE (verb)	to lower in dignity; to destroy the independence of; to subdue, crush, or break; to mortify, degrade or shame; to make inadequate or unworthy

If that is what humility means, who would want to be humble? Here's the bad news: *God* wants us to be humble. What's the good news? The good news is that the definitions listed above are not God's definition of humility.

God is not confined by society's attitude; he *values* humility. In fact, the first step to *having* a relationship with God is humbling oneself. It is also the first step to *restoring* a broken relationship with God. Anyone who has struggled with an addiction knows this truth: the first step is to admit there is a problem. That is where humility comes in. We have to be willing to admit that we have a problem, acknowledge that we cannot fix our own problems and ask for help. This is the kind of humility that God is looking for, the kind he honors.

Since the Bible was written in two different languages, there are two different words for *humble*. The Hebrew word is *kana*. It means "to be humble, subdued, brought down, brought into subjection." The Greek word is *tapeinoo*, which means, "to lower; to bring down one's pride, have a modest opinion of oneself, or behave in an unassuming manner."

Notice the difference between the Bible's definition and the dictionary definitions listed above. The Bible teaches a lowering of one's pride and opinion – but it is a lowering, not a crushing. God does not want to crush our spirits or degrade us in any way. He is out to humble us, not to humiliate us.

However, God will see us humbled. The Hebrew word for *humble* in 2 Chronicles 7:14 is in the *niphal verb tense*. *Niphal* can be either a *passive* verb or a reflexive verb. *Passive* means that it is *done to you* instead of you doing it yourself. *Reflexive* is approximately the opposite: it means you *do an action to yourself.* So, how can a verb be both passive and reflexive?

This occurs when humility is a choice. We can humble ourselves (reflexive), or God will humble us (passive). But one way or the other, we will be humbled. Perhaps that sounds cruel. How can a God who claims to love us and treasure us also want to humble us? Luke 20:18 tells us, "Whosoever shall fall upon that stone shall be broken; but on whomsoever it shall fall, it will grind him to powder." This means that if we humble ourselves and fall upon the Lord, who is the rock referred to in this verse, then we will be broken, but not destroyed; broken, but re-buildable into his likeness. But if we do not choose to humble ourselves, then he, the Lord, must do it...and the breaking will be much more severe. Either way, it is for our benefit that it must be done, but so much the better if done by our own choosing.

First, remember that God wants humility and not humiliation. He does not shame us, crush us or force us into submission. Quite the opposite: God removes our shame and guilt. He gives us purity and joy. Instead of making us plain and common, God calls us to a life that is different, a life that is abundant and free. God wants us to see the potential that we have in him. He wants us to come to a place where all things are possible because we are living in the power of Christ. That is the desire of his heart but that can only come through humility and utter dependence on him.

Second, God demands humility because he alone is worthy of praise and glory. Maybe it is not quite right in our minds but God is God. A king has the right to demand respect from his subjects, and there is no greater king than God Almighty. He refuses to share his throne with anyone or anything. Not only that, but he would be doing us a disservice to let us claim any praise or glory that does not rightfully belong to us.

There is also another reason for us to choose humility. It is right for us to humble ourselves because God humbled himself. Psalm 113:4-6 says:

> *The LORD is high above all nations, his glory above the heavens. Who is like the LORD our God, who dwells on high, who humbles himself to behold the things that are in the heavens and in the earth?*

Do we realize that every time God looks at us, he first humbles himself? Every time God listens to our prayers he lowers himself to do so. That is not meant to demean us so please don't take it the wrong way. God is so huge and so high that every interaction with mankind is a humbling experience for him, an act of condescension in the true sense of the word. We often put a negative connotation to the word, "condescension." When we accuse someone of being condescending to us, we have the idea that they are talking down to us because they think they are "better than us" or "above us." But God actually is above us. He truly is higher than us, and therefore must condescend, or humble himself, lower himself down to our level, if he is to communicate with us at all. But he is willing to humble himself because he loves us that much. If the God of the universe humbles himself for us, doesn't it make sense that we should humble ourselves for him? In our case, it is only an acknowledgement of our position before him.

Jesus also humbled himself for us. Philippians 2:5-11 says:

> *Let this mind be in you which was also in Christ Jesus, who, being in the form of God, did not consider it robbery to be equal with God, but made himself of no reputation, taking the form of a bondservant, and coming in the likeness of men. And being found in appearance as a man, he humbled himself and became obedient to the point of death, even the death of the cross. Therefore God also has highly exalted him and given*

him the name which is above every name, that at the name of Jesus every knee should bow, of those in heaven, and of those on earth, and of those under the earth, and that every tongue should confess that Jesus Christ is Lord, to the glory of God the Father.

Jesus ruined his reputation for us. Jesus was and is God. Though he could have claimed his rights as God, he instead gave up those rights so that we could have eternal life. Even while being beaten and mocked for no reason, Jesus refused to claim his rights. Peter says, "when he was reviled, he did not revile in return; when he suffered, he did not threaten, but committed himself to him who judges righteously" (1 Peter 2:23). Jesus knew that he was acting in obedience to God, so he laid down his rights and his life. He condescended to us because of his great love for us.

Now, he asks us to do the same. Jesus asks us for the same humility, but he also offers us the same reward. When Jesus lowered himself in obedience to God the Father, the Father lifted him up to a place of honor. Jesus promises us the same thing:

Humble yourselves in the sight of the Lord, and he will lift you up. (James 4:10)

Humble yourselves under the mighty hand of God, that he may exalt you in due time. (1 Peter 5:6)

Jesus promises us a place of honor if we are willing to humble ourselves but there is an even better reward than that. More desirable than honor, Jesus offers grace to the humble:

Surely he scorns the scornful, but gives grace to the humble. (Proverbs 3:34)

For thus says the High and Lofty One who inhabits eternity, whose name is Holy: "I dwell in the high and holy place, with him who has a contrite and humble spirit, to revive the spirit of the humble, and to revive the heart of the contrite ones." (Isaiah 57:15)

There is honor in humility, but there is also grace, forgiveness and fellowship with God in humility. God desires brokenness from his people – brokenness over sin and rebellion. He promises forgiveness, restoration and life to anyone who is willing to humble him or herself enough to ask for it.

What does humility look like? How does one live a humble life in the eyes of God?

First, remember that humility is a process, not a one-time fix. The verb *humble* in 2 Chronicles 7:14 is in the *niphal* tense, but it is also in the *imperfect* tense. The imperfect tense is a *continual* tense; it refers to the process more than the fact and emphasizes frequent repetition. The natural human tendency leans toward pride. Pride is what got the devil kicked out of heaven. It is our first and strongest sin, so it is the hardest to overcome. We cannot go to sleep proud and wake up humble the next day. It is not that simple. It is not that easy. Humility takes effort – continual, repeated effort. A constant effort to remember who we are and what we are; and a constant effort to strive to be who and what God wants us to be.

Second, look for ways to put other people first. Paul encouraged the Philippians:

> *Let nothing be done through selfish ambition or conceit, but in lowliness of mind let each esteem others better than himself. Let each of you look out not only for his own interests, but also for the interests of others. (Philippians 2:3-4)*

The Bible does not say we cannot consider our own interests at all but that we also need to look out for other people's interests. So, the next time we feel the urge to demand our own way, take a step back and put someone else's needs first. Back down in an argument. Listen instead of talking. Make a phone call or send a card. Pray. Let someone else choose where to eat. Simple little things can make a world of difference.

Finally, when we feel the need to compare ourselves to others, compare ourselves to Jesus instead. Ask God for a realistic self-view. God can help us see who we really are. He will help us see how our sin breaks his heart – how filthy it is in his eyes. He will help us see how small our life is, how inconsequential it is on the timeline of eternity. It is hard to puff oneself up when up against the God of the universe.

God will help us see ourselves as he sees us. He will show us that we are his beloved children and friends. He will recall to us all the times he has come through for us simply because he loves us. He created us and wrote a fabulous life story for us. He shed his blood to save us. He put his Spirit in us to guide us and to comfort us.

God promised us that we can do all things (Philippians 4:13) – that nothing is impossible – if we just believe. He has given gifts (Romans 12:4-8; 1 Corinthians 12, 14; 1 Peter 4:9-11) and talents (Genesis 4:21-22), likes and abilities (Genesis 25:27), passions and dreams (Joel 2:28) so that he can use us to do amazing things for his Kingdom.

Finding the balance between these two self-images is the key to living a life of humility. Focusing too much on the first leads to depression and a sense of futility. Focusing too much on the second leads to arrogance and a sense of divine entitlement. The truth is somewhere in the middle. Of course our sin makes us "scum," but scum that is dearly loved by Almighty God. He loves us in spite of ourselves. He passionately and unconditionally loves us, not because we deserve it.

Quite frankly, we don't. He loves us because he is good. He does it because he wants to.

Even with these teachings, examples and promises, we are often still so unwilling to lower ourselves. Almighty God will humble himself for us, but we cannot bring ourselves to do the same. We will not admit defeat. We will not admit error. We will not ask for forgiveness or help. We will not trust him to fix the mess we have made for ourselves. We will not praise Him because we are so busy seeking our own praise. We simply refuse. Why is that?

Your Turn

1. How would you define the word HUMBLE or HUMILITY?

   _____

   _____

   _____

   _____

   _____

2. Why is humility necessary to having a relationship with God?

   _____

   _____

   _____

   _____

3. How does it make you feel to know that God would never humiliate you?

   _____

   _____

   _____

   _____

4. How does it make you feel to know that God/Jesus humbled himself for you?

    _____

    _____

    _____

    _____

    _____

5. Do you have a hard time humbling yourself before God? What about before other people? Why do you have such a hard time lowering yourself?

    _____

    _____

    _____

    _____

    _____

Chapter 6:

Pray

When We Pray We Follow God's Will

Prayer is the *greatest gift* God could give us. Prayer is talking to God, plain and simple; and yet, that is the most profound truth imaginable. When we pray, we have the full attention of Almighty God. The Creator of the universe focuses on us. We get to talk to him like we would talk to our spouse, parent or friend. Through Jesus' saving grace, we have unlimited and an undeniable access to God and every right to take advantage of that gift, as well as every right to expect results from those prayers. This is assuming, of course, that we are doing it his way. James 5:16 tells us that, "The effectual fervent prayer of a righteous man availeth much." *Effectual* is defined as something that is sufficient or able to produce a desired effect, meaning that it has the qualities and power behind it to produce that effect. *Fervent* is something of great zeal or intensity. So an effectual, fervent prayer, then, would be one that is prayed with sufficient power behind it, coupled with great intensity and passion in the person praying. These types of prayers avail much, or produce much result. Does this mean that we must always passionately cry out and beg God for what we want or need? No. There are times for that, certainly, but the passion in our hearts toward a particular subject is already known to him. As we discussed earlier though, in speaking about humility, it does help to put things into perspective for us about who has the need and Who has the power to meet that need, doesn't it?

Prayer is also the *most effective tool* that God has given us. When we pray in his Spirit and according to his will, nothing can stop those prayers from being heard and answered. Prayer causes Satan to tremble and causes demons to flee.

However, prayer is also perhaps the *most misunderstood gift* of the Christian life. Since it is so misunderstood, it is also the *most unused tool* available to Christians. Why is that? Bible commentator David Guzik said, "Prayer is so simple that the smallest child can do it, but it is so great that the mightiest man of God cannot be said to truly have mastered prayer." The more we learn about prayer, the more we realize we have a lot to learn.

> Prayer is so simple that the smallest child can do it, but it is so great that the mightiest man of God cannot be said to truly have mastered prayer.
>
> –David Guzik

People are mistaken when they make procedural rules for prayer: *say this, do this, but only do it on these days or at these times or in these locations, etc.* That is not God's intention for prayer. God wants a relationship with us and he invites us to bring our concerns, thoughts, needs, desires and issues to him. He does not care *when* we pray or *where* we pray; he simply desires that we *pray.*

However, there are some *guidelines* for prayer in the Bible. These are not rules; rather they are advice to help us see how God wants to be approached.

Prayer is a Command

I exhort therefore, that, first of all, supplications, prayers, intercessions, and giving of thanks, be made for all men; For kings, and for all that are in authority; that we may lead a quiet and peaceable life in all godliness and honesty. For this is good and acceptable in the sight of God our Savior; Who will have all men to be saved, and to come unto the knowledge of the truth. For there is one God, and one mediator between God and men, the man Christ Jesus; Who gave himself a ransom for all, to be testified in due time. Whereunto I am ordained a preacher, and an apostle, (I speak the truth in Christ, and lie not;) a teacher of the Gentiles in faith and verity. I will therefore that men pray everywhere, lifting up holy hands, without wrath and doubting. In like manner also…women … (1 Timothy 2:1-9)

First and foremost, God wants us to pray. God commands us to talk to him because he wants a relationship with us. Prayer is not a command in the sense that it is a law that cannot be broken. Instead, it is more of a principle.

We cannot have a relationship if we do not have communication. Imagine a friendship where the friends never spoke. Or consider a marriage where the spouses never communicated. Relationships are nonexistent without communication. If this is true in our human relationships, then it is even truer in our relationship with God.

Prayer is More Than Asking for Stuff

And Moses returned unto the LORD, and said, Oh, this people have sinned a great sin, and have made them gods of gold. Yet now, if thou wilt forgive their sin--; and if not, blot me, I pray thee, out of thy book which thou hast written. (Exodus 32:31-32)

The Hebrew word for *pray* in 2 Chronicles 7:14 is *palal*, which means, "to intervene, interpose, mediate, or intercede." When we pray, we act as a go-between God and people. However, the verb is in the *hithpael* tense. That particular tense can be reflexive, but it can also be *reciprocal.* In laymen's terms, that means *God commands us to pray for ourselves (reflexive) and to pray for one another (reciprocal).*

Jesus' model for prayer is entirely couched in exactly those terms. It is a conditional covenant:

> *After this manner therefore pray ye: Our Father which art in heaven, Hallowed be thy name.*
> *Thy kingdom come, Thy will be done in earth, as it is in heaven.*
> *Give us this day our daily bread.*
> *And forgive us our debts, as we forgive our debtors.*
> *And lead us not into temptation, but deliver us from evil: For thine is the kingdom, and the power, and the glory, forever. Amen. (Matthew 6:9-12)*

Notice that the first thing Jesus models is to pray for God's *holiness,* after acknowledging his holiness. We ask for a qualification to enter God's presence. That is something he must do *for* us. This is what gives us the power behind the prayer mentioned earlier in regard to the word effectual.

Next we make our biggest, most important requests: (1) That his ultimate victory over sin, his Kingdom to come, will hurry; and (2) That his perfect will (salvation) will be accomplished on earth, the way it is in Heaven. For everyone in Heaven, salvation is a *done deal.*

Next, we ask for his day-by-day supply. That's the way Jesus said to ask for it. Keep in mind, he commanded us to *ask* for it every day, so it obviously doesn't bother God to give it. By asking for it on a daily basis, (1) we acknowledge that everything comes from him, and (2) we participate in the supplication. Asking for God's provision daily helps to grow our faith because we are continually learning to trust that he will provide for us today just as he did yesterday.

Now comes the clearest example of *reciprocation* in prayer: *forgive us our debts as we forgive our debtors.* That can be understood as "forgive us in proportion to our forgiving." We cannot expect mercy without being merciful.

Next we ask for protection. "God," we pray, "Please don't let me go anywhere near evil or temptation." This is the equivalent of being "in the world, but not of the world." Because we encounter evil everywhere we go, there is no escape from the temptations of Satan. They are in us. Just as Paul wrote in Romans, there is none righteous, no not one. So, again, we have to ask God for his righteousness so we won't trifle with it or become enamored with it.

Finally, we acknowledge the whole purpose of our being: "It's your Kingdom. It's your Authority. It's your Glory. *Forever.*" That's the part of our prayer in which we acknowledge God's eternal purpose - to bring his creation into relationship with himself.

If we're not careful we can look at this prayer and mentally check off the aspects that we have rightfully mentioned. This would be the wrong attitude because prayer is so much more than a shopping list! Prayer, at its very heart, is a relationship with God.

Prayer Involves God

But what saith it? The word is nigh thee, even in thy mouth, and in thy heart: that is, the word of faith, which we preach; That if thou shalt confess with thy mouth the Lord Jesus, and shalt believe in thine heart that God hath raised him from the dead, thou shalt be saved. For with the heart man believeth unto righteousness; and with the mouth confession is made unto salvation. For the scripture saith, Whosoever believeth on him shall not be ashamed. For there is no difference between the Jew and the Greek: for the same Lord over all is rich unto all that call upon him. For whosoever shall call upon the name of the Lord shall be saved. (Romans 10:8-13)

The first involvement anyone can have with God is praying for salvation. Paul argues that salvation is available through one avenue: *calling on the Name of the Lord in faith.* From that point on, the Christian has access to God's involvement. We are *being saved* (continual action), and we must fervently involve God in our lives if we are to continue the change he wants to make in our lives.

Salvation is God's perfect will for our lives. Do we want to know *exactly* what God wants from us? Do we want to know *exactly* what God wants? He wants *relationship* with the lost, and he wants *partnership* with the saved.

Prayer Involves Persistence

Rejoice evermore. Pray without ceasing. In every thing give thanks: for this is the will of God in Christ Jesus concerning you. Quench not the Spirit. (1 Thessalonians 5:16-19)

Since *pray* is in the imperfect tense, prayer should be a *continual act.* Notice the continual/comprehensive action expressions in this passage: *evermore, without ceasing, everything is, concerning, quench not.* Prayer is to go on and on, but not because God is stubborn or hesitant to answer. In fact, Jesus says that just the opposite is true:

And he spake a parable unto them to this end, that men ought always to pray, and not to faint; Saying, There was in a city a judge, which feared not God, neither regarded man: And there was a widow in that city; and she came unto him, saying, Avenge me of mine adversary. And he would not for a while: but afterward he said within himself, "Though I fear not God, nor regard man; Yet because this widow troubleth me, I will avenge her, lest by her continual coming she weary me."

And the Lord said, Hear what the unjust judge saith. And shall not God avenge his own elect, which cry day and night unto him, though he bear long with them? I tell you that he will avenge them speedily. Nevertheless when the Son of man cometh, shall he find faith on the earth? (Luke 18:1-8)

Imagine a wife who is constantly nagging at her husband to do more around the house. Eventually the husband will take out the trash not because his desire is to serve his wife, but because he believes that's the only way to turn her nagging off! Too many times people feel that they are nagging God when they continually ask for the same things over and over. We do not nag God because God *does* care. He *does* want to hear from us. When he senses the urgency in our prayers and our commitment, he answers speedily.

If that is the case, why does prayer take so long? Frankly, answered prayers can be sparse because we don't always ask God for the right thing. We haven't always identified or understood our problem correctly. The more time we spend with God, the more clearly we understand *what* we are to pray for. Prayer doesn't take so long because God takes a long time to answer; it sometimes takes a long time because *we* often need a long time to understand what we are asking ffor.

Prayer Involves Power

Seek the LORD, and his strength: seek his face evermore. (Psalm 105:4)

How are we to find His strength? It seems to be wrapped up in seeking the Lord. The book of James addresses how that is possible:

Confess your faults one to another, and pray one for another, that ye may be healed. The effectual fervent prayer of a righteous man availeth much. Elias was a man subject to like passions as we are, and he prayed earnestly that it might not rain: and it rained not on the earth by the space of three years and six months. And he prayed again, and the heaven gave rain, and the earth brought forth her fruit. Brethren, if any of you do err from the truth, and one convert him; Let him know, that he which converteth the sinner from the error of his way shall save a soul from death, and shall hide a multitude of sins. (James 5:16-20)

Here's some startling news: the key to power in prayer is *confession*. It is the prayer of a *righteous* person that makes a big difference. Righteousness is not something we call up from within. According to the prophet Isaiah, "there is none righteous, no, not one." (Psalm 14:1-4; Romans 3:10). Righteousness comes from God. It is "imputed" (Romans 4:6-11). To *impute* means to *assign*. In other words, God puts us in charge of righteousness when we come to him in confession. It is our *First Commission*, before the *Great Commission*. Every believer has 2 jobs: (1) to care for the righteousness *imputed* to them by God, and (2) to *impute* the Gospel message to others so they can receive Christ in faith and confession.

> THE KEY TO POWER IN PRAYER IS CONFESSION

Prayer is a direct result of a salvation relationship with God where we are actively seeking his face. It is through our relationship with the Holy God that we become righteous. According to James, it is in the *righteousness* assigned to us by God that *power* is found in prayer. According to James, the greatest power we can exert in prayer is turning someone else from his or her sin. There it is - the *First Commission* <u>empowers</u> the *Great Commission*.

Prayer Includes Promises

He that spared not his own Son, but delivered him up for us all, how shall he not with him also freely give us all things? (Romans 8:32)

Salvation is the greatest thing in the world, a seal of God's continuing benevolence toward us.

That we should be to the praise of his glory, who first trusted in Christ. In whom ye also trusted, after that ye heard the word of truth, the gospel of your salvation: in whom also after that ye believed, ye were sealed with that holy Spirit of promise, Which is the earnest of our inheritance until the redemption of the purchased possession, unto the praise of his glory. (Ephesians 1:12-14)

Paul was an empiricist. In his opinion, God's willingness to see his Son crucified in our stead should be all the proof we should ever need that he will hear our prayers and meet our needs. The forgiveness of our sin, along with the Holy Spirit's dwelling in our hearts after receiving Christ by faith, should be all the proof we would ever need that God will answer our prayers.

The Bible contains a countless number of scriptures that demonstrate God's sealed promises related to prayer. Let's consider a few of them here:

1   *Prayer is conditioned on faith.*

   And all things, whatsoever ye shall ask in prayer, believing, ye shall receive. (Matthew 21:22)

The key to prayer is trusting in God's goodness. Society trains us to be paranoid, but Satan enhances our paranoia by calling things to our attention that seem to prove that God is untrustworthy. Faith in Christ for salvation and for supply, sanctification and safety is necessary for our prayers to have any strength.

2   *God hears our prayers of faith.*

   Hear me when I call, O God of my righteousness: thou hast enlarged me when I was in distress; have mercy upon me, and hear my prayer. O ye sons of men, how long will ye turn my glory into shame? How long will ye love vanity, and seek after leasing? Selah. But know that the LORD hath set apart him that is godly for himself: the LORD will hear when I call unto him. Stand in awe, and sin not: commune with your own heart upon your bed, and be still. Selah. Offer the sacrifices of righteousness, and put your trust in the LORD. There be many that say, who will shew us any good? LORD, lift thou up the light of thy countenance upon us. Thou hast put gladness in my heart, more than in the time that their corn and their wine increased. I will both lay me down in peace, and sleep: for thou, LORD, only makest me dwell in safety. (Psalm 4)

In an era of information overload where parents spend more time on e-mail, Facebook, Twitter and Google than they do talking with their children, it is difficult to believe that God actually pays any attention to each of us individually. When Jesus raised Lazarus from the dead, He said:

Father, I thank You that You have heard Me. And I know that you always hear me. (John 11:41-42)

We have this same guarantee if we pray in the same way Jesus did, in a relationship of absolute trust, that God will hear our prayers.

3   God will give in response to prayers of faith.

Trust in the LORD with all your heart, and lean not on your own understanding; In all your ways acknowledge him, and he shall direct your paths. Do not be wise in your own eyes; fear the LORD and depart from evil. It will be health to your flesh, and strength to your bones. Honor the LORD with your possessions, and with the firstfruits of all your increase;
So your barns will be filled with plenty, and your vats will overflow with new wine. My son, do not despise the chastening of the LORD, nor detest His correction; For whom the LORD loves He corrects, just as a father the son in whom he delights. (Proverbs 3:5-12)

Economics, like all life issues, generally result in two reactions: (1) We cling even closer to God; or (2) We doubt God's goodness.

Notice the descriptions Solomon offers of *trusting in the Lord with all your heart*: don't count on your own understanding (*...Thy will be done*); pay attention to his nature in every decision (*...Thy Kingdom come*); don't get an overblown opinion of our own cleverness (*...in earth, as it is in Heaven*); be appropriately respectful of his power (*...hallowed be Thy Name*); stay away from shortcuts and evil options (*...lead us not into temptation, but deliver us from evil*); honor him with all that we have and with everything we produce (*...for Thine is the Kingdom and the power and the glory forever. Amen.*); and pay attention when he corrects our direction (*...our Father, which art in Heaven*).

As a result of these acts of obedience, he gives us direction (*forgive us our debts*); he guards our health (*as we forgive our debtors*); we'll have plenty to take care of, even to the point of overflowing (*give us this day our daily bread*). God is love. God is a giver. It is his nature.

4   *God is motivated when he answers prayers of faith.*

And whatsoever ye shall ask in my name, that will I do, that the Father may be glorified in the Son. If ye shall ask any thing in my name, I will do it. (John 14:13-14)

Asking in Christ's Name is a testimony that we have placed our faith in Jesus for salvation. God answers those prayers because Jesus is glorified when we are holy "name-droppers." When Christ's Name is used, God gets excited. Someone is bragging on his Son.

We Don't Get Because We Don't Ask.

If it is true that God is motivated to answer prayers of faith, then why aren't all prayers answered? The classic text on this subject is found in

James 4:2: *You have not because you ask not.* That is not the end of the teaching, although that's where the quotation usually ends. As with 2 Chronicles 7:14, we fail to look at the context - probably because this little quote is so *riveting.* It sounds so wonderful as a stand-alone thought: "The only reason I don't get what I want is because I don't ask for it! Yay!"

If that was all, wouldn't it be great? However, James doesn't stop there. More importantly, he didn't *start* there. James 4:2 is near the conclusion of a larger discourse concerning our *speech habits,* beginning with James 3:1. Let's look at the entire passage.

1   Our prayer will be unfocused if the rest of our speech is chaotic (3:1-2).

> *My brethren, be not many masters, knowing that we shall receive the greater condemnation. For in many things we offend all. If any man offend not in word, the same is a perfect man, and able also to bridle the whole body.*

James goes so far as to say that, if a person controls his speech, the rest of his character will be complete. That is quite a statement but it really isn't that surprising. Faith is dependent upon *the Word,* so it is not surprising that prayer would hinge on *our words.*

2   Speech is a control issue (3:3-4).

> *Behold, we put bits in the horses' mouths that they may obey us; and we turn about their whole body. Behold also the ships, which though they be so great, and are driven of fierce winds, yet are they turned about with a very small helm, whithersoever the governor listeth.*

A bridle controls a horse. A rudder determines the course of a ship. James' implication is obvious - the outcome of our lives is determined by our manner of speech.

3   Our words have consequences, both good and bad (3:5-8).

> *Even so the tongue is a little member, and boasteth great things. Behold, how great a matter a little fire kindleth! And the tongue is a fire, a world of iniquity: so is the tongue among our members, that it defileth the whole body, and setteth on fire the course of nature; and it is set on fire of hell. For every kind of beasts, and of birds, and of serpents, and of things in the sea, is tamed, and hath been tamed of mankind: But the tongue can no man tame; it is an unruly evil, full of deadly poison.*

If we do not control our mouths, it proves we have no self-control. According to Christ, our speech reveals our true nature. "...of the abundance of the heart his mouth speaketh" (Luke 6:45).

4   Our words produce a schizophrenic prayer life (3:9-12).

> *Therewith bless we God, even the Father; and therewith curse we men, which are made after the similitude of God. Out of the same mouth proceedeth blessing and cursing. My brethren, these things ought not so to be. Doth a fountain send forth at the same place sweet water and bitter? Can the fig tree, my brethren, bear olive berries? Either a vine, figs? So can no fountain both yield salt water and fresh.*

How can purity come out of a sewer? How can sweet blessings come out of the same bucket as bitter cursings? And how can prayer come from a mouth that condemns and complains? The answer is obvious: these things can't happen. Sincere prayer requires us to make a choice: are we going to live for God or the world?

5   Our words eventually flesh out in actions (3:13-18).

Who is a wise man and endued with knowledge among you? Let him shew out of a good conversation his works with meekness of wisdom. But if ye have bitter envying and strife in your hearts, glory not, and lie not against the truth. This wisdom descendeth not from above, but is earthly, sensual, devilish. For where envying and strife is, there is confusion and every evil work. But the wisdom that is from above is first pure, then peaceable, gentle, and easy to be intreated, full of mercy and good fruits, without partiality, and without hypocrisy. And the fruit of righteousness is sown in peace of them that make peace.

Sooner or later, we get tired of being "all talk." Someone calls our hand and we have to put up or shut up. Or, like Abraham and Sarah, we get tired of waiting on God to keep his promise and decide to keep his promise for him. That leads us to cut corners, make exceptions and operate in the "gray" areas of faith and life.

5   We substitute our poverty for God's plenty (4:1-2).

From whence come wars and fightings among you? come they not hence, even of your lusts that war in your members? Ye lust, and have not: ye kill, and desire to have, and cannot obtain: ye fight and war, yet ye have not, because ye ask not.

Here's the verse we've been waiting on. *Why don't we get what we need?* We don't get what we need because we don't ask for it. *Why don't we ask for it?* We don't ask, because we'd rather do it ourselves. If we're honest, experience proves this to be true.

Since my mouth is out of control, and I feel rather helpless in that regard, I compensate by grasping control of my decisions. God is a lot smarter than me, and that's hard to accept. He's invisible after all, and sometimes that's just creepy. If I ask, he might say *no.* So, rather than wait, rather than be insecure, I try to do it myself. I might make a mess, but it will be *my* mess. I'll be in control of my chaos.

6   We substitute our wants for God's will (4:3-6).

Ye ask, and receive not, because ye ask amiss, that ye may consume it upon your lusts. Ye adulterers and adulteresses, know ye not that the friendship of the world is enmity with God? Whosoever therefore will be a friend of the world is the enemy of God. Do ye think that the scripture saith in vain, the spirit that dwelleth in us lusteth to envy? But he giveth more grace. Wherefore he saith, God resisteth the proud, but giveth grace unto the humble.

It's not so much that we ask for the wrong things, as it is that we ask for the wrong reasons. The wrong reason is *lust*. We approach prayer with the attitude of: I want what I want when I want it. We've just stood before a holy God with the morality level of a two-year-old! The primary block to prayer therefore is *idolatry*. When we pray for what *we* want, that is *self-worship*. *Prayer is about what God wants*. That leads us to James' problem-solving section of his discourse about getting prayer answered:

7   Find out what God wants (4:7-10)

Submit yourselves therefore to God. Resist the devil, and he will flee from you. Draw nigh to God, and he will draw nigh to you. Cleanse your hands, ye sinners; and purify your hearts, ye double minded. Be afflicted, and mourn, and weep: let your laughter be turned to mourning, and your joy to heaviness. Humble yourselves in the sight of the Lord, and he shall lift you up.

THE PRIMARY BLOCK TO PRAYER IS *IDOLATRY*

How do we do that? How can anyone ever really know the will of God? James was open about this. As we've seen so far, our prayers are hindered by the unholy content of our mouths. To speak to God, we must be holy. To hear God, we must be holy. It is a matter of holiness. James gives us some steps to know the will of God:

- *Submit yourself to God (7a).*

  This is the most anti-idolatry thing a follower of Christ could possibly do. Prayer is not just asking God to give us things or telling God all of our problems. Prayer is doxology, praise, thanksgiving, confession, supplication and intercession to God. The common term used for prayer for those with a Yiddish background is to *daven* (pronounced *daa-ven*). Some say that *daven* comes from the Hebrew word *dovaiv*, which means "to move the lips." *Davening* is when Jews move their lips. They don't pray silently; they pray verbally, vocalizing their prayers. It is a visible communication with their master. It is submission through communication.

- *Resist temptation (7b).*

  If we do that, Satan will run away scared. Bullies aren't used to getting punched in the nose. We do not realize that he has given us power over the works of the enemy. Therefore, we have to come to an understanding as to who we are in Christ and then walk in it. The Word *authority* means the "lawful right to enforce obedience and to give orders." It is our legal right to enforce God's order on earth.

- *Get as close to God as possible (8a).*

  We must make sure we are praying from the right (heavenly) position and posture (unmoved, able, sure-footed and confident.) When we pray from the right position and the right posture we are given the right perspective.

- *Cleanse your deeds (8b).*

  Jesus' earthly ministry demonstrates how to conduct our lives. He showed us how to exercise power over the flesh. We were created in his image, according to his likeness. Moreover, the same Spirit that lived in him lives in us. We are usually too busy living life in our old nature to grasp who we are in God. We should not act and live as if we are still under Satan's control (Ephesians 2:1-6).[36]

- *Purify your heart of double-mindedness (two-faced thinking) (8c).*
  Proverbs 29:2 reminds readers when the righteous are in authority, the people rejoice. For too long Christians have been operating beneath their station. That is one reason Satan has had such success operating above his. It is time for the church to stand up and be counted. Christians have been sidelined for too long and have allowed the enemy to have his way. We complain that the Bible is not allowed in schools but fail to realize that we are walking epistles read by all men. No one could successfully take the Bible out of school if believers entered the school with the Word of God active and alive within them.

- *Take sin seriously (9).*
  Satan has a system and structure in operation on earth and in the demonic kingdom that this world follows. Demons take dominion over human bodies that have opened themselves up to their influence. Demons influence humans with lies, enticing words, the lusts of the flesh and eye and the pride of life (1 John 2:16).

- *Humble yourself so God can be the one who glorifies (boasts about) you (10).*

---

[36] [1]And you hath he quickened, who were dead in trespasses and sins; [2]Wherein in time past ye walked according to the course of this world, according to the prince of the power of the air, the spirit that now worketh in the children of disobedience: [3]Among whom also we all had our conversation in times past in the lusts of our flesh, fulfilling the desires of the flesh and of the mind; and were by nature the children of wrath, even as others. [4]But God, who is rich in mercy, for his great love wherewith he loved us, [5]Even when we were dead in sins, hath quickened us together with Christ, (by grace ye are saved;) [6]And hath raised us up together, and made us sit together in heavenly places in Christ Jesus:

The Bible says in Ephesians 2:6 that he (God) raised us up together with him and made us sit down together giving us joint seating with him in heavenly places. This being the case, we then, have to understand that we are seated above demonic influence. Therefore, our spiritual posture should be where we are seated -- not where we are standing. Let that one sink in for a minute. Re-read it if you need to. Once we are in Christ, we are above principalities and powers. We are above demons and any and all types of spirits. Luke 10:17 says that God has given us authority and power to trample upon serpents and scorpions and over all the power of the enemy and nothing shall by any means hurt us. Because we have the same spirit in us that was in Christ Jesus when he was in his earthly ministry, so we can do greater works!

God Plans to Win.

Finally, my brethren, be strong in the Lord, and in the power of his might. Put on the whole armor of God, that ye may be able to stand against the wiles of the devil. For we wrestle not against flesh and blood, but against principalities, against powers, against the rulers of the darkness of this world, against spiritual wickedness in high places. Wherefore take unto you the whole armor of God, that ye may be able to withstand in the evil day, and having done all, to stand. Stand therefore, having your loins girt about with truth, and having on the breastplate of righteousness; And your feet shod with the preparation of the gospel of peace; Above all, taking the shield of faith, wherewith ye shall be able to quench all the fiery darts of the wicked. And take the helmet of salvation, and the sword of the Spirit, which is the word of God: Praying always with all prayer and supplication in the Spirit, and watching thereunto with all perseverance and supplication for all saints. (Ephesians 6:10-18)

No one wins the war with sin by accident; only warriors win. We are called to be warriors in the battle between heaven and hell and our greatest warfare takes place in prayer. We are called to be "prayer warriors."

The only way to become skilled prayer warri0rs is to join in the battle. We will either pray our way through it, or give in to the attacks. It's up to us. David learned how to deal with attacks and opposition while tending sheep. He killed a lion and a bear before he defeated Goliath. Before we can face and fight our Goliath we must face the lions and bears that enter our lives to cause us to question our calling. After those first victories, David began to walk in power and authority while in the battle with Goliath. "Praise be to the LORD my Rock, who trains my hands for war, my fingers for battle" (Psalm 144: 1).

David did not wait until he had a reputation as a warrior or until he became king. Unfortunately, the church tends to wait for earthly influence before we walk in power, or else we simply wait until it is too late to do anything before we want to start walking in authority. If we are to possess the power of God by faith we must use it. Faith without works is dead.

David had valor, power and authority. He was unafraid to face his enemy head on. He capitalized on his shepherding experiences. He was willing to defend God's Name, God's Kingdom, God's leaders and God's people. We must be willing to serve and protect at all costs. Spiritual authority doesn't come just because we say we are saved. Demons are not afraid of that. Demons pester us during worship. They sing in our choirs, preach in our pulpits, tell us they love us and can speak in unknown tongues. A demon is only afraid

> NO ONE WINS THE WAR WITH SIN BY ACCIDENT

of the believer who knows who they are in Christ, has taken his spiritual position and is not afraid to boldly walk in it.

In Luke 18: 1-2, Jesus taught that believers ought to always pray and not turn coward (lose heart, faint or give up). In other words, no matter what situations arise, believers don't run away and cry. Satan is always plotting and planning the demise of the saints; we can't get rid of him. However, according to James, we can kick him out.

It is our responsibility to go to war for our purpose and our destiny by using God's Word! We win this battle by the armor that God has provided (Ephesians 6:10-18). Using the sword of the Spirit (the Word of God), we can pray the promise instead of praying the problem.

Look at God's strategy for dealing with the chaos Satan brought into the world. The Bible says in Genesis 1 that the earth was without form and void and darkness hovered over the face of the deep. That word *form* in Greek is *huw - to lie waste, a desolation of surface i.e. desert worthless thing, confusion.* The cosmos had no structure or order. When Satan was cast out of heaven the Lord used the Word of God to re-establish his order on the earth (Revelation 12:7-9).[37]

In Genesis 1:1 when humanity fell out of the will of God, God used his Word to reset the order. When Satan tried to tempt Jesus after His 40-day fast in the wilderness, (Matthew 4: 1-11) Christ used the Word of God to defeat him. It is the power of the spoken Word of God that *we* release from our mouths that will infect the world and enforce change. The Bible says that death and life is in the power of the tongue and those that love it will eat of its fruit (Proverbs 18:21).

---

[37] Revelation 12:7-9 [7]And there was war in heaven: Michael and his angels fought against the dragon; and the dragon fought and his angels, [8]And prevailed not; neither was their place found any more in heaven. [9]And the great dragon was cast out, that old serpent, called the Devil, and Satan, which deceiveth the whole world: he was cast out into the earth, and his angels were cast out with him.

Satan will be slain by our Lord Jesus Christ, by the breath of his mouth, his word, and by the brightness of his coming and his anointing (2 Thessalonians 2:8). The Word empowers our prayers. It is the substance of our prayers. The Bible says that we should *make* our prayers unto him (God) in the name of Jesus and he will hear us (John 14:13-14). That word *makes* means to *compose, construct or design.* We are to pray in such a way that our prayers are composed, constructed, designed and fashioned after, and according to the Word of God.

> *HOLINESS* IS THE KEY TO ANSWERED PRAYER

When we use anointed words we literally stop the gates of hell from prevailing. This means that the believer armed with faith in Jesus Christ can storm hell, kick down its gates, and rescue those prisoners shackled within.

> *And I say also unto thee, That thou art Peter, and upon this rock I will build my church; and the gates of hell shall not prevail against it. (Matthew 16:18)*

Not only can we storm hell, but we also have the keys to heaven. This speaks of our authority in prayer.

> *And I will give unto thee the keys of the kingdom of heaven: and whatsoever thou shalt bind on earth shall be bound in heaven: and whatsoever thou shalt loose on earth shall be loosed in heaven. (Matthew 16:19).*

God gives us authority and power through the Holy Spirit of God to lock and to unlock. In other words, whatever we release on earth, God will release in heaven and whatever we lock down on earth God will lock down in heaven. We are God's earthly representatives and so whatever we allow, God allows. Conversely, whatever we disallow God disallows. The only way God will hear our prayers is if it is in accordance with his word (1 John 5:14).

God is calling out those who will seek him in Spirit and in truth, and who will stand and take their place with God. The level of our prayer life is a clear reflection of our relationship with God. As Christians, we have become weak. We have left our post as soldiers of Christ. We have lost our focus and have substituted religious tradition for the will of God. A spirit of repentance is necessary before we will see the power of God made manifest. When Daniel received the news that God was bringing judgment on the nation of Israel he set out to understand what that meant, and began to pray and repent - not just for the Jews, but also for himself.

> *I set my face unto the Lord God, to seek by prayer and supplications, with fasting, and sackcloth, and ashes... (Daniel 9:3)*

Holiness is the key to answered prayer.

> *When the righteous are in authority, the people rejoice: but when the wicked beareth rule, the people mourn. (Proverbs 19:2)*

Leaders and all those in authority over others must be uncompromisingly righteous if the authority is to be sound and if the people are to rejoice. James promised, "The effectual fervent prayer of a *righteous* man availeth much"(James 5:16). That is, the prayer of a holy man makes a difference. It gets results as discussed earlier. The earnest, heartfelt continued prayer of a righteous man, a man in right standing with God, makes tremendous power available. The secret to power of prayer is having a pure heart before God.

Obviously, this power comes at a personal cost. It is not for use by the token believer or careless disciples.

> *The sacrifices of God are a broken spirit: a broken and a contrite heart, O God, thou wilt not despise... (Psalm 51:17).*

No one said as much about the mechanics of prayer as Jesus himself. Mark reports these bullet points about effectual praying from our Lord:

> *For verily I say unto you, That whosoever shall say unto this mountain, Be thou removed, and be thou cast into the sea; and shall not doubt in his heart, but shall believe that those things which he saith shall come to pass; he shall have whatsoever he saith. Therefore I say unto you, What things soever ye desire, when ye pray, believe that ye receive them, and ye shall have them. And when ye stand praying, forgive, if ye have ought against any: that your Father also which is in heaven may forgive you your trespasses. But if ye do not forgive, neither will your Father which is in heaven forgive your trespasses. (Mark 11:23-26)*

Jesus taught that if we pray in faith, whatever we ask will be granted. However, this receipt is contingent upon believing that we will receive what we asked for. James told the believers facing tribulation that a double-minded man can't receive anything from the Lord (James 1:6-8). However, it is important to understand the context. James was teaching about asking for wisdom - a more or less guaranteed prayer request, as long as the petitioner had faith in God's goodness in giving. This promise is not carte blanche to ask for *anything*. A holy person will, by implication, seek wisdom from God when he prays.

The Hebrew word for prayer is *tefilah*. The word is a derivative of the word *pellel*, which means, "to judge." *Tefilah* is a time of self-evaluation, self-judgment, and introspection. It is when a person takes the time to focus on himself and look within to see what he is all about, what his faults are, what his qualities are, what he needs from God and why God should give it to him. This self-assessment process happens through *tefilah*.

Another translation is "attachment." When we *daven* (pray), we create a bond with our Creator. *Prayer is a process of putting things together.* The secret to God answering our prayers is having a pure heart before him. It is what we mean by *integrity,* or having a "knit-together" character. We have come before God in an attitude of introspection, longing for a deeper relationship with Christ. Then our prayers will matter.

YOUR TURN

1. Why did God command you to pray?

_____

_____

_____

_____

_____

_____

2. How can you improve your prayer life?

_____

_____

_____

_____

_____

_____

3. What is the key to answered prayer?

_____

_____

_____

_____

_____

_____

4. What are the blessings tied to prayer?

_____

_____

_____

_____

_____

_____

Chapter 7:

Seek His Face

When We Seek His Face, We Enjoy God's Presence

God promised healing and blessing if we seek him. Seeking God is important because we have an overwhelming need to worship him. The process of praying is to seek the face of God, to get his attention, to get to know him personally. God wants us to enter his throne room with confidence, to bow down before him and experience his holiness. When we experience God's holiness, we will admit and proclaim that there is none like him.

God wants us to realize who he is. Knowing the names of God will help develop a more intimate relationship with him. We looked at some of those names earlier, but let's review them briefly:

El Elyon	"The Most High God" stresses his strength, sovereignty and supremacy
El Olam	"The Everlasting God" emphasizes his unchangeableness and is connected with his inexhaustibleness
El Shaddai	"God Almighty" names him as the One who corrects and chastens
Yehovah-Yireh	"The Lord who Provides" stresses his provision for his people
Yehovah-Nissi	"The Lord Your Banner" presents him as our rallying point and means of victory; the One who fights for his people
Yehovah-Shalom	"The Lord our Peace" points to him as the means of our peace

	and rest
Yehovah-Shammah	"The Lord who is There" reveals his personal presence
Yehovah-Tsidkenu	"The Lord our Righteousness" portrays him as the means of our righteousness
Yehovah Sabbaoth	"The Lord of Hosts" presents him as commander of the armies of heaven
Yeahovah Maccaddeshcem	"The Lord your Sanctifier" shows that he is our means of sanctification; he sets believers apart for his purposes
Yeahovah Roi	"The Lord my Shepherd" pictures him caring for his people as a shepherd cares for the sheep of his pasture
Theos	"God" is the primary name for him in the New Testament.
Kurios	"Lord" implies authority and supremacy; the equivalent of Yehovah. It too is used of Jesus Christ meaning Rabbi, Sir, God or Deity
Despotes	"Master" carries the idea of ownership
Abba	"Father" stresses God's loving care, provision, discipline, and the way we are to address God in prayer

Seek in Hebrew is *baqash* , which means "to seek in order to find, secure, to seek the face, desire, require, ask, request, strive after, examine through touching." The verb is in the *piel imperfect* tense.

The *piel* tense means it is intensive, or intentional. It is a distinction of degrees from the *qal* verbs. An example would be the idea of someone breaking a dish. The *qal* sense of the word is simply "He broke the dish," whereas the *piel* rendering of the verb would translate to "He smashed the dish."

The *imperfect form* implies continual action. The breaker of the dish isn't finished. He keeps breaking dish after dish, stomping and grinding the dishes that are already broken, and when he runs out of dishes in his cupboard, he looks for whatever else in the house he can smash and breaks those things too. He is either crazy, furious, out of control or is getting paid to break as many dishes as he can in 20 minutes. You get the idea.

> WE SEEK GOD'S
> FACE BECAUSE
> WE GRASP WHAT
> LIFE IS LIKE
> WITHOUT HIM

Now, apply this to *seeking* God's face. Being told to, "Keep your eyes open for a sale on dishes when you are at the mall", illustrates the *qal* tense. You may have dishes in mind but if something else comes along that interests you more than dishes, you will have no trouble shifting your focus to that.

The *piel* tense can be illustrated like this: imagine a mother and her three-year-old daughter at the mall. They stop at the food court to buy an ice cream cone. The mother pays for it, the vendor hands it to her, she turns to give it to her daughter and discovers that the toddler is gone. She scans the crowd frantically, trying to find the child's tiny face. She can't find her in the food court, so she runs outside, throwing the cone in the trash, her head whipping back and forth, looking far and fast, hoping to glimpse her t-shirt or ponytail. She sees a security guard and rushes to him, describing her daughter. The guard gets on the radio and alerts all of mall security. An announcement goes out over the intercom. The mother is in tears, already picturing her family's reaction to the news that their baby girl is gone, already feeling the guilt and grief.

Then the guard begins asking questions. *Do you bring your daughter here a lot? What's her favorite thing to do here?* She thinks frantically and remembers she always wants to look at the puppies in the front window of the pet store. The guard speaks into his radio, listens for a moment, and then turns to her with a grin. "She's at the pet store. One of our guards is standing beside her."

The mother sprints for the pet store not stopping until she sees her little girl with her nose against the glass of the pet shop window, unaware of the stir she has caused. She lifts her into her arms and cries. She has no idea why she was interrupted but she hugs her mother and then innocently wants to know where her ice cream is.

That's the difference between *qal* seeking and *piel* seeking. We are to seek God frantically, not casually. We look for him desperately, not with unconcern. We exhaust all resources seeking God's face because we grasp what life is like without Him. This type of seeking is demonstrated by the word "desire" in Daniel 2:18 where Daniel goes before the Lord to inquire about the dream. However, Daniel wants more than a simple interpretation of the king's dream, but wants to know what the dream itself was. The king could not even remember what he had dreamed.

The king had ordered all of the wise men of Babylon to be put to death because no one could tell him what he had dreamed, nor what it meant. Daniel, being the only one of the wise men in the land who knew the One True God of heaven, found himself and his three friends needing to go before the Lord and *piel* seek answers from God. The need for answers was intensified by the fact that the lives of all the wise men of the land were at stake. Because of Daniel and his friends' willingness to *piel* seek, to inquire and to search until answers were found, lives were literally spared. This is the picture of intensity in seeking we must grasp if we are to truly seek God's face.

The Hebrew word for *face* is *paniym*, which can also mean "presence." An idol is no more the reality of God than an abstract drawing is the reality of my mother. A picture is okay, but I want her presence. As John said,

> *Beloved, now are we the sons of God, and it doth not yet appear what we shall be: but we know that, when he shall appear, we shall be like him; for we shall see him*

as he is. And every man that hath this hope in him purifieth himself, even as he is pure. (1 John 3:2-3)

There it is again - *holiness*. If we want to see God, we must be holy. If we want our prayer to matter, we must be holy.

Why do we need to be holy? Because he is holy; and holiness can only be in the presence of holiness. So we must be holy if we want to enter into his presence because any un-holiness cannot be in the presence of holiness. Therefore, if we want to be in his presence we must do away with anything that will prevent our ability to do so. It is the ONLY way to be in the presence of God. God's greatest desire is to spend time with his children. Holiness is the only way to do that.

In his wisdom, God allows what he can easily prevent by his power. If we can rise above circumstances and the worldly things that steal our time and attention, if we can be quiet and seek his face and if we will listen for his still, small voice, he will impart greater revelation of his kingdom and his purposes.

God is calling us to a time of clarity in what we see and hear. However, we must come into the realm of the Spirit and refuse to allow fleshly desires to pervert the purity of what he is about to impart. This place of holiness will require sanctification and consecration. We must give ourselves wholly, fully and completely to the Lord.

If you feel you relationship with God is where it needs to be, then this chapter is for someone else. This chapter is for those who desire to be real before the Lord today, and confess that they have allowed the cares of this world to take their attention from God. God deserves our whole attention. It is a "must" for our lives.

So we bow as we enter the throne room and we cast ourselves down at your feet.

We cry holy, thou art holy, there is none like thee. In Your presence is where we must be. [38]

Worship is an intricate part of seeking God. God created us to worship him. Our worship to God is an expression of our love, gratitude and appreciation for who he is and what he has done for us. Knowing who the Father is during our time of worship will allow us to develop a personal bond with our Creator.

When was the last time you worshiped God and genuinely enjoyed being in his presence? You see, it is in the presence of God, in his *face,* that you will see changes and miracles. It is in the presence of God that lives are transformed. It is in the presence of God that deliverance takes place. It is in the presence of God that marriages are healed and restored. It is in his presence that people see themselves for who they really are.

When you seek him, truly and honestly seek him, laying down all earthly thoughts, activities and desires, holding nothing back from him, all the entanglements of this life will fall away. They will become so insignificant that they all but disappear. It is only in this state that you will be able to enter into the presence of his face; and it is there that you will have the privilege of dwelling, for as long as you so choose, in his holy presence.

David wrote, "When you said, 'Seek my face,' my heart said unto You, 'Your face Lord, will I seek'" (Psalm 27:8). The word *seek* is a translation of the Greek word *zhteite* —which means, "having an urgency, a desire and an ambition for something. [39] The body of

---

[38] Shekina Glory Ministry, *Before the Throne*
[39] http://www.firstbaptistchurchoc.org/Articles/a_twofold_challenge.htm

Christ, and we, as individuals, are called to go after, pursue and enter into the presence of God. We are called to seek him, not merely with lip service or even acts of service, but with our hearts. Somewhere along the line, we have lost our passion to seek the face of God. We have become so consumed with the cares of this world that our focus has taken a shift.

Martha was in the same position. She and her sister Mary were quite literally in the presence of the Lord. They both had the same opportunity available to them to sit at Jesus' feet and learn from him:

> *Now it came to pass, as they went, that he entered into a certain village: and a certain woman named Martha received him into her house. And she had a sister called Mary, which also sat at Jesus' feet, and heard his word. But Martha was cumbered about much serving, and came to him, and said, Lord, dost thou not care that my sister hath left me to serve alone? Bid her therefore that she help me.*

> *And Jesus answered and said unto her, Martha, Martha, thou art careful and troubled about many things: But one thing is needful: and Mary hath chosen that good part, which shall not be taken away from her. (Luke 10:38-42)*

Martha made the decision to serve in the natural and Mary made the decision to serve in the spiritual (worship the Lord). Neither was wrong, but Jesus told Mary that she had "chosen that good part, which shall not be taken from her" (Luke 10:42). Serving God in the natural or doing good works as a result of our faith in God should still never take the place of our worship of him. The enemy devises distractions to shift our attention away from God. We become busy, consumed with our family, children and work or we spend a great deal of our time watching television.

Some may be thinking right now, "But I am *blessed.*"

Yes, we have blessings in our life. Yes, favor may be flowing in our life.

Yes, we are blessed - but at what cost? What did we have to surrender for these blessings? What sacrifice was made in order to receive the blessing and favor?

As I examine my own life, I can see where a distraction has come to keep me busy with the cares of this world. The enemy's desire is for us to neglect God and others. The spirit of neglect is so powerful and so cunning that if we are not careful we will fall into its trap. Some signs of neglect include: a lack of desire, no prayer or very little, complacency, laziness, frustration or selfishness. It can be easy to see ourselves in this list!

We are guilty of neglect when we give insufficient attention to something. This can be hard to detect because we tend to think that we are okay and doing just fine spiritually. That is the enemy's strategy - to keep us in denial. As long as we are in denial we will never get past our present state.

Neglect occurs when we forget to fulfill our obligations or duties. God created us to do something he does not do for himself: worship him. It is our duty to worship and have fellowship with God. When a husband or wife gives more attention to their friends than their own spouse, that's neglect. No one likes to feel neglected, yet we offer it to God on a daily basis. We give more attention to other people or things than to the One who created them.
God wants us to seek his face. He desires to spend time with us. He wants nothing more than for his children to recognize their need of him. He is a loving, tender and gracious Father who wants to spend time with his children, but he will not beg, threaten or coerce his children to spend time with him. He will simply not bless us with his presence if we choose not to seek him. We are the ones who suffer

when we choose to neglect our relationship with God. He misses us, but he will not force himself on us. But his holiness does require that he refrain from blessing us as much as he would like to because we are distracted with other things and are not responsible enough to have those blessings. If you think you are blessed now, imagine how much MORE you could be blessed if you increased your time spent with your heavenly father. Wow! Just imagine it!

If My people, who are called by My name, shall humble themselves, pray, seek, crave, and require of necessity My face and turn from their wicked ways, then will I hear from heaven, forgive their sin, and heal their land (2 Chronicles 7:14, Amplified Bible).

The only way we can begin to seek the Lord is by following his requirements

- Humble ourselves
- Pray
- Seek his face
- Turn from our wicked ways

At the beginning of his ministry, the prophet Isaiah received one of the most glorious visions of God ever given to a human being. Isaiah saw the Lord sitting upon a throne, magnificent and lifted up:

In the year that king Uzziah died I saw also the LORD sitting upon a throne, high and lifted up, and his train filled the temple. Above it stood the seraphims: each one had six wings; with twain he covered his face, and with twain he covered his feet, and with twain he did fly. And one cried unto another, and said, Holy, holy, holy, is the LORD of hosts: the whole earth is full of his glory. And the posts of the door moved at the voice of him that cried, and the house was filled with smoke. (Isaiah 6:1-4)

Isaiah understood that he was in a place with God that he had never been to before. Humility in prayer will take us to places in God that we have never experienced.

Then said I, Woe is me! for I am undone; because I am a man of unclean lips, and I dwell in the midst of a people of unclean lips: for mine eyes have seen the King, the LORD of hosts. (Isaiah 6:5)

It was in God's presence that Isaiah was able to see himself for who he truly was. Isaiah was able to see that he was a man of unclean lips. He was able to confess his sins before the Lord. When we seek God's face and realize who he is, only then can we see who we are.

Then flew one of the seraphims unto me, having a live coal in his hand, which he had taken with the tongs from off the altar: And he laid it upon my mouth, and said, Lo, this hath touched thy lips; and thine iniquity is taken away, and thy sin purged. (Isaiah 6:6-7.)

Folks, God is calling for a people that will seek his face. We cannot turn from our wicked ways until we seek the face of God. We cannot progress until we seek him. It's our seeking, thirsting, and craving for God that allows us to progress and find the peace, spiritual enrichment and fulfillment we have been searching for.

When Peter, James and John received a veiled glimpse of the face of God on the Mount of Transfiguration, they did the one thing they had never done before: they fell facedown to the ground in reverence and in acknowledgement of the presence of God (Matthew 17:4-8). Are we willing to bow down and worship the Lord like this? Are we willing to give up the things that are so readily available to us in this world and which distract us from pursuing God's presence with everything within us on a regular basis? Do we *really* want to know God? Those who make the sacrifice of time and effort,– and in reality, *take* the time (from other things) to worship the Lord –will not be disappointed.

YOUR TURN

1. Why is worship so important?

_____

_____

_____

_____

_____

_____

2. Why were you created for worship?

_____

_____

_____

_____

_____

3. How can worship affect your relationship with God?

_____

_____

_____

_____

_____

_____

4. What is worship to you?

    _____

    _____

    _____

    _____

    _____

    _____

Chapter 8:

Turn From Wicked Ways

When We Turn From Wicked Ways, We Obey God's Commands

For the final chapter, we will spend time in brief word studies. Three words dominate this final clause of God's conditions for restoration: *turn, wicked* and *ways*.

Turn

The Hebrew word is *shuwb*, meaning "to return, to turn back, repent/to turn away, repel/ to bring back, restore/ to give back, relinquish/ to pay back, recompense." It has a broad use in scripture and depending on the context, this word can be translated *break, build, circumcise, dig, do anything, do evil, feed,* or *lay down.*

It is a primitive root. Strong's Exhaustive Bible Concordance supplies an additional translation and application of the word: to turn back, literally or figuratively, but not necessarily with the idea of returning to the starting point.[40]

It is written in the *Qal imperfect* tense. As noted above, *Qal* makes it an *active* verb. The Old Testament use of *shuwb* in *Qal* tense has these renderings:

[40] Strong's Exhaustive Concordance- online. http://strongsnumbers.com/hebrew/7725.htm

1) to turn back, return: a) to turn back; b) to return, come or go back; c) to return unto, go back, come back; d) of dying; e) of human relations (fig); f) of spiritual relations (fig); 1) to turn back (from God), apostatize; 2) to turn away (of God); 3) to turn back (to God), repent; 4) turn back (from evil).[41]

Imperfect makes it a verb of continual action. Where this word is used, it specifies a turning away that doesn't stop.

So, turn, and keep on turning; that is, once you've chosen your new direction, keep going in that direction. Christ considered this an imperative of discipleship.

> *And another also said, Lord, I will follow thee; but let me first go bid them farewell, which are at home at my house.*
> *⁶And Jesus said unto him, No man, having put his hand to the plough, and looking back, is fit for the kingdom of God. (Luke 9:61-62)*

Wicked

The second big word is the Hebrew word *ra,* which means "bad, evil, displeasing, hurtful, injurious, wrong, worse, sad." In various scriptural contexts, *ra* is the noun form of the verb root *ra'a,* meaning: "Be so bad, badness, be so evil, naughtiness, sadness, sorrow, wickedness."

The short definition of this verb is *afflict.* It can mean, "to spoil by breaking to pieces, to make (or be) good for nothing, to do harm, to hurt.[42]

---

[41] http://biblelexicon.org/2_chronicles/7-14.htm
[42] http://strongsnumbers.com/hebrew/7489.htm

The wickedness of any person leaves evidence. Jesus applied this idea vividly in Luke 6:43-45, speaking of evidence in the kind of fruit a person's life produces:

> *For a good tree bringeth not forth corrupt fruit; neither doth a corrupt tree bring forth good fruit. For every tree is known by his own fruit. For of thorns men do not gather figs, nor of a bramble bush gather they grapes. A good man out of the good treasure of his heart bringeth forth that which is good; and an evil man out of the evil treasure of his heart bringeth forth that which is evil: for of the abundance of the heart his mouth speaketh. (Luke 6:43-44)*

God cannot bless wickedness. He can only bless obedience to his Word. Proverbs 28:13 tells us, "He that covereth his sins shall not prosper: but whoso confesseth and forsaketh them shall have mercy." This means that if we try to cover our wickedness and make ourselves believe that God 'didn't notice it,' or we hope he will look the other way, God's blessings are withdrawn from us. In fact, he tells us in his Word "...be sure your sin will find you out" (Num. 32:23). But if we repent, or *turn from* our wickedness, then God's lavish blessings can once again be ours. This is his desire for us.

James adds to this thought with his discussion of how hypocrisy corrupts speech among believers:

> *Out of the same mouth proceedeth blessing and cursing. My brethren, these things ought not so to be. Doth a fountain send forth at the same place sweet water and bitter? Can the fig tree, my brethren, bear olive berries? Either a vine, figs? So can no fountain both yield salt water and fresh. Who is a wise man and endued with knowledge among you? Let him shew out of a good conversation his works with meekness of wisdom. But if ye have bitter envying and strife in your hearts, glory not, and lie not against the truth. This wisdom descendeth not from above, but is earthly, sensual, devilish. For where envying and strife is, there is confusion and every evil work. But the wisdom that is from above is first pure, then peaceable, gentle, and easy to be intreated, full of mercy and good fruits, without partiality, and without*

hypocrisy. *And the fruit of righteousness is sown in peace of them that make peace.* (James 3:12-18)

Ways

Ways is another Hebrew noun, *derek*, meaning "road, journey, direction, manner, habit, course of life." This is in keeping with the thought of continually turning from our wickedness. We are in essence choosing a different path, continually turning away from the wickedness that is set before us by our enemy.

Definitions include: actions, acts, conduct, course, crooked, direction, distance, example, favors, highway, highway, impulses, journey, line, manner, mission, path, pathless, pathway, pathway, practice, road, roads, roadway, safely, street, toward, toward, walk, way, way in the direction, way toward, ways, wayside, wherever.[43]

It comes from a verb root, *darak,* which can mean aimed, bend, treading, walk and wielding.

Humanity's bent toward self-destruction is revealed in a person's way: "There is a way which seemeth right unto a man, but the end thereof are the ways of death" (Proverbs 14:12). The goal for anyone's ways is the acknowledgement of their integrity: "By mercy and truth iniquity is purged: and by the fear of the LORD men depart from evil. When a man's ways please the LORD, he maketh even his enemies to be at peace with him" (Proverbs 16:6-7). The first test for anyman's ways (manner of life) is faith in God: "Trust in the LORD with all thine heart; and lean not unto thine own understanding. In all thy ways acknowledge him, and he shall direct thy paths" (Proverbs 3:5-6).

Behavioral scientists tell us that habits are difficult to break because habits fill a felt need. When the person attempts to stop a particular habit, it leaves a "hole" in their heart. They need something to fill that void. Cigarettes, candy, food, exercise, entertainment, sex, drugs, liquor, or hobbies - we could go on and on with the things we try to stuff in that gaping hole. Not all of them are bad - they just can't fill the hole. What can do it?

Get a new *way*. Where we go and how we get there makes all the difference in the world. Jesus claims that for himself.

> *"I am the way, the truth, and the life: no man cometh unto the Father, but by me." (John 14:16)*

If you have had a major change in your life in recent weeks or months, be warned that there will be things offered to you by the Devil himself that will appear to fill the void created by this change. It could be a change of habit if you tried to quit smoking, or go on a major diet; or it could be something like a death, divorce or other loss in your life. These are prime opportunities for Satan to plant a seed in the minds of God's children to desire things of this life that will distract them from God. Don't be a victim of his ploys to steal you away from your God. Keep your eyes on God by keeping your *ways* turned toward him. He will bless you in tremendous ways if you are steadfast in your commitment to walk in his ways.

The Lord God wants everyone to partake in the lavish blessing; however, it is only available to those who have been called by his name. The beauty about being called is that it is available to everyone who believes. The Bible says in Romans 10:9-10, "...that if thou shalt confess with thy mouth the Lord Jesus, and shalt believe in thine heart that God hath raised him from the dead, thou shalt be saved.

For with the heart man believeth unto righteousness; and with the mouth confession is made unto salvation."

The Lord loves us so much that he has given us the opportunity to receive Jesus Christ as Lord and Savior right where we are. If you are interested in being a part of the Kingdom of God and desire to partake in the lavish blessing that has been made available to us, then I want you to pray this simple but powerful prayer from your heart and mean it with all of your heart:

> *Lord Jesus, Here I am, just the way that I am. I believe in you and I believe you have died for me and that you have risen again and one day you're coming back to receive me unto yourself. Lord Jesus, please forgive my sins and all of my transgressions and save my soul from an eternity in hell. I receive you Jesus as Lord and Savior; thank you for saving me, as I accept the free gift of salvation.*

> *Thank you for forgiving me my sins and saving my soul.*

Let me be clear here. These words are not a magic potion and have no saving power in and of themselves. They are an expression of a sinful soul to a holy God. If you prayed them, maybe not the *exact* words, but the sentiment related by them, and you *meant* it with all of your heart and understood what it means, then let me be the first to say: ***welcome to the family!***

Conclusion

What does it mean to live under the lavish blessing of God?

 We have his attention.

 We have his acceptance.

 We have his abundance.

What "sacrifice" is required for us to have the perpetual blessing of God in our life?

  We must honor his name.

  We must display his glory.

  We must follow his will.

  We must enjoy his presence.

  We must obey his commands.

So, what do we think? Is the wage worth the work? Is the payment worth the price? Is the reward worth the sacrifice?

Perhaps we look at that outline and it makes perfect sense. Perhaps we have discovered that knowing God is worth any effort, sacrifice or price. If so, jump into a lavish relationship with him.

However, perhaps we still are not convinced. Perhaps we look at the list above and feel like it is unfair – that God is asking too much from us. Before we make our choice, consider these points.

First, God is God. That means he doesn't owe us anything – not even an explanation. He can demand any action he wants from us, simply because he is the Sovereign Ruler of the universe. He can expect our obedience for the same reason.

However, God does not operate that way because of his lavish love. So, *while God can demand anything he wants, he chose these requirements because they make sense.* His requests are logical. God's IF statements are not his way of being mean or demanding – he does not want to withhold the THEN blessings. He requires these actions because they are necessary.

To experience God's attention, we must honor his name, display his glory, follow his will, enjoy his presence and obey his commands. God loves us enough to pay attention to us even when we dishonor and disobey him. But we will not enjoy or appreciate his attention if we are doing those things. How can he hear us if I we not praying to him? How can he get me if I am not willing to humble myself enough to be honest with him?

To experience God's acceptance, we must honor his name, display his glory, follow his will, enjoy his presence and obey his commands. This is a tricky one, because we have God's acceptance the moment we accept Jesus as Lord. He already atoned for our sins and he adopted us into his family the exact second that we said yes to his gift of salvation. But we will not experience and enjoy that acceptance if we are not growing closer to God. We have his acceptance regardless of our actions, but that acceptance will not be a reality in our life if we spend our life dishonoring and disobeying God.

To experience God's abundance, we must honor his name, display his glory, follow his will, enjoy his presence and obey his commands. We have the ability to stand firm, but first we must realize that we stand in his strength. We have the ability to stand free, but first we must humble ourselves and admit our need of him. We have the ability to stand full, but first we must acknowledge that God is the only thing we need in life.

But here's the good news: *this doesn't have to happen overnight.* Living in God's lavish blessing is really about having a relationship with him –

and relationships take time. Notice a progression in God's requirements. It is a deepening relationship. First, believe in his grace and the sacrifice of Jesus Christ. Next, allow God to work and show his glory. Finally, surrender to his will. As we do those things, we will fall in love with him, earnestly seeking his face and his presence. Then once we have given our heart and soul to the God of the universe, we will want to obey his commands and his plan for our life. It's a relationship, an ever-growing, ever-deepening relationship.

God pours out his blessing each step of the way. When we accept his salvation and begin wearing his name, then he will give us his attention, acceptance and abundance. When we take the next step and allow him to display his glory in us, he will give us more of his attention, acceptance, and abundance.

About the Author

Living a blessed life is not about how much money you have or the many degrees you may have earned. Living a blessed life is about embracing the promises God has made available to every believer through Christ Jesus. Every Christian can live a blessed life that has been created by God if they are willing to follow God's plan.

Dr. Hood is the co-founder along with her husband Bishop D.G. Hood of The Enrichment Center in Fort. Lauderdale, Florida. She is also a Licensed Marriage and Family Therapist, Motivational Speaker, adjunct professor, and Mother. Dr. Hood has dedicated her life to helping others view their circumstances from different vantage points so that they can focus on God's unique plan of destiny for their lives.

www.ingramcontent.com/pod-product-compliance
Lightning Source LLC
Chambersburg PA
CBHW031513040426
42445CB00009B/215

* 9 780578 449722 *